D0934584

TRENDS IN BUSINESS ETHICS

To Lenny and Brita

NIJENRODE STUDIES IN BUSINESS

Volume 3

Business is a broad field where science and business reality can and should meet to analyse and discuss old theories and to develop new ones, applicable for modern managers. One of the main objectives of the **Nijenrode studies in business** is to give a push to new developments in the multidisciplinary business area, to serve the profession as well as a wider audience.

Trends in business ethics

Implications for decision-making

Cees van Dam and Luud M. Stallaert

editors

Martinus Nijhoff Social Sciences Division
Leiden/Boston 1978

Distributors for North America
Kluwer Boston Inc.
160 Old Derby Street
Hingham, MA 02043 USA

ISBN 90.207.691.8

Printed in the Netherlands.

PREFACE

In August 1976 the research seminar 'Decision-making in business' was organized at Nijenrode, The Netherlands School of Business. More than fifty scientists and practitioners from nine countries presented research papers in one of the six discussion groups. Some of them also presented some of their ideas in front of a large mixed audience at a one-day symposium. Many of the papers presented at Nijenrode were of such a high quality that the decision to publish a selection of them was an easy one. At the same time the new series *Nijenrode studies in business* was initiated. All who were involved, the policy committee of the *Nijenrode studies*, the advisory and editorial board of the series, the publisher, and the organizing committee of the seminar and symposium, acclaimed the idea of publishing three volumes in the new series. A collection of eleven papers could be grouped under the title *Trends in managerial and financial accounting*, and has been published as volume 1 of this series. A collection of fourteen papers has been published as the second volume under the title *Trends in financial decision-making*, while this volume, consisting of twelve papers (and an introduction) explores the theme *Trends in business ethics*.

The introduction by *Stanley L. Jaki* was written for the symposium. It suggests why the papers of Pjotr Hesseling, Antoine Kreykamp, and Richard H. Viola, which were not presented at Nijenrode, are introduced here. They were invited to elaborate within the frame of the themes of the seminar on aspects that had been proven to be useful.

Pjotr Hesseling gives some reflections on the nature of the confrontation between multinationals and developing countries. He suggests an intermediate set of practical requirements between a universal level and personal responsibility – a challenge for those in the field of business ethics.

In his paper, *Antoine Kreykamp* relates technology to ethics. The problems of ethics transcend those of technology; they are not problems concerning restricted fields, but relate to being as a whole. Our minds have to be broadened to see what is, in reality, of greater importance.

In a both history- and philosophy-oriented paper, *Richard H. Viola* accentuates the human values. Business is in a phase of transition; if it is to keep its leading place in society (and it should), it must be recognized as an open system, not one which is only market oriented. Management has to take steps to make the corporation 'a channel through which its employees can manoeuver on their way to full expression of newly acquired values.'

The books are intended for those who are interested in new developments in the decision-making area. They are especially suitable for graduate or advanced undergraduate courses: volume 1 in managerial or financial accounting courses; volume 2 in courses on managerial finance, capital budgeting or decision-making; and volume 3 in courses on business ethics, business policy or related fields.

Many people have contributed to the success of the seminar and the symposium and made it possible for these three books to be published. In the first place, the authors of the papers who were all willing, not only to write a paper, but also to present it at Nijenrode, to discuss it with critical colleagues, and last but not least to revise it according to the capricious ideas of the editors. My thanks to all of them. But the whole enterprise would not have gotten off the ground without the great support of the members of the organizing committee of the seminar and symposium. As the president of that committee I have never made a vain appeal to any of the members. Because I am not able, nor do I wish, to discriminate between them, I will give their names in alphabetical order: Peter Hesp, Piet Koeleman, Luud Stallaert and Tony de Wit. Of course, much had to be arranged, but the committee had dependable help in the person of Sybren Tijmstra, who was always there to bring the organizing committee down to earth. Many secretaries have made extra effort, but one of them in particular has to be mentioned because of her continuous enthusiasm before, during and after the symposium and seminar: Josée Terheggen. She did a wonderful job. Of course without the moral and financial support of the Board and different committees of Nijenrode all preparations would have led to nothing. I look back and still appreciate the year of enormous effort which went into the preparations for the congress.

It is hoped that the first three volumes of the series *Nijenrode studies in business* will be received with as much enthusiasm outside Nijenrode as was always present within the group of people who have made it all possible.

Cees van Dam

CONTENTS

Contributors to the volume

PJOTR HESSELING, Professor of Organization and Management at Erasmus University, Faculty of Economics, Rotterdam, The Netherlands.

ARIJ HORDIJK, Secretary-General of the Dutch Confederation of Christian Trade Unions (CNV), Utrecht, The Netherlands.

STANLEY L. JAKI, Distinguished Professor at Seton Hall University, South Orange, New Jersey, U.S.A.

ANTOINE KREYKAMP, Civil servant engaged in problems of adult education, Amersfoort, The Netherlands.

JOHAN C. RAMAER, Manager of the Bureau for External Economic Relations of N.V. Philips' Gloeilampenfabrieken, Eindhoven, The Netherlands.

WILLEM L. VAN REIJEN, Associate Professor of Social Philosophy at the State University Utrecht, Department of Philosophy, Utrecht, The Netherlands.

HEIN SCHREUDER, Head of business research at the Economic and Social Institute of the Free University, Amsterdam, The Netherlands.

LUUD M. STALLAERT, Associate Professor of Methodology and Business Ethics at Nijenrode, The Netherlands School of Business, Breukelen, The Netherlands.

CHRISTIAAN H. I. E. M. TEULINGS, Member of the executive board of VNU (United Dutch Publishers), Haarlem, The Netherlands.

R. SYBREN TIJMSTRA, Assistant of the President of Nijenrode, The Netherlands School of Business, Breukelen, The Netherlands.

RICHARD H. VIOLA, Professor of Management and Organizational Behavior at Temple University, School of Business Administration, Philadelphia, Pennsylvania, U.S.A.

MAURICE A. M. DE WACHTER, Associate Professor of Medical Ethics, University of Nijmegen, School of Medicine and Dentistry, Nijmegen, The Netherlands.

I. DECISION-MAKING IN BUSINESS: AMORAL?

Stanley L. Jaki

The papers which follow, focusing on business decisions and ethics, most taken from a conference on that subject, show clearly that they were written by people who seek after truth very earnestly. This is the first point to be made, a point of no small matter nowadays when in most conferences – and their number is increasing by leaps and bounds – the prevailing attitude is to score easy points while leaving the difficult and fundamental questions untouched. The second point is that these papers cover a wide range of topics. Indeed, they seem to cover all the basic approaches that can be taken to the topic of ethics in business decisions. Had the topics of these papers been chosen randomly there would undoubtedly have been some duplication approaching a Gaussian distribution. Instead we have a distribution resembling a straight horizontal line, hardly a matter of chance.

Indeed, we owe it to Stallaert's careful planning and foresight that the topics of the papers do not reveal the slightest trace of fusion, if not confusion, which is always the outcome when random factors are at work.

In thinking nowadays about ethics in business, one's very first thought is led to business firms, especially to large corporations, which set the pace of modern business enterprise. Two of the papers, one by Teulings, another by Ramaer, have these business entities for their subject matter but in such a way as to forestall duplication. Teulings' principal concern is the structure of a business firm insofar as it is susceptible to ethical responsibility, or rather as it can be the carrier of such responsibility. The structure is, as is well known, a complicated set of sub-ordinated and co-ordinated managerial, decisional, marketing, advertising, and executive organs, which can easily lead to the erosion of the sense of ethical responsibility. The process is known, to use the American idiom, as 'passing the buck,' a process which might seem satisfactory or at least tolerable at one time or another, but hardly in our times. Ours is an age, as Teulings points it out with great force, which is saddled with a keen awareness of ethical responsibility. As causes for the rise of that awareness Teulings points at the atrocities committed against the Jews and the plight that was caused by the war in Vietnam.

Undoubtedly, he did not mean to be exclusive. The twentieth century has witnessed so many other plights as to easily deserve the sad distinction of being the century of genocide. It makes a sad reflection on our ethical insensitivity that we in the free Western world are not more upset than we are by the horrendous toll which Marxist dictatorships, hunger, and disease are taking in many places on the globe. In view of this one cannot help asking whether, as Teulings gravely notes, it is really humane or ethical on the part of a business corporation to pour luxury items into underdeveloped countries. The procedure implies making profit by playing on the human craving for luxury with the result that scarce money is being syphoned away from funds needed to secure basic necessities of life. Another example is the marketing of inefficient drugs, which relies on the proverbial desire to regain health at any price, even at the price of plain folly. Clearly such business ventures are abuses against honesty and will not be prevented unless a set of ethical principles is spelled out within the company itself. Such are some of the reasons which compel Teulings to assert the principle of what he calls 'intrinsic company responsibility' and to call for the formulation of explicit standards of business ethics. Or as the conclusion of his paper states: 'Society demands that the company, as an important social institution, act with a sense of ethical responsibility and publicly proclaim its standards, dare to defend them and dare to let them be used as a touchstone for its actions.'

Quite similar is the conclusion reached by Ramaer, whose paper relates to a special if not chief characteristic of modern business, the role of multinationals. As everybody knows, multinationals dominate the pulse of economic life, of economic fate and fortunes. Their decisions heavily influence social peace which, as Ramaer points out, 'implies mutual respect and consent,' but these in turn cannot be had 'if there is no common ground in the form of certain values considered worth pursuing.' Since Ramaer deals with multinationals as private enterprises, he first considers the basic ambitions, duties, and rights of man as an individual, then he gives a list of considerations about man as a social being, with an emphasis on his relation to the state and to economic life. What is particularly informative in his paper is related to the parallel which he draws between a non-international and an international enterprise. While a non-international firm has in a sense to cope only with the ethical standards of a given society or nation, the international firm seemingly has no such concern because of the wide differences in ethical norms across nations, differences that may serve as convenient excuses for disregarding those very same norms. A good illustration of this is the question of bribe. It is an open secret that in many parts of the world bribing is an accepted way of doing business. Should not this fact absolve multinationals based in the United States of any wrongdoing? Are not they entitled to reject or disregard American legal rules against bribing as fossil remains of a so-called blue-nosed ethic which is no longer accepted even in the United States by the majority of the people? Are not those American-based multinationals right in arguing that if they discontinue bribing, they would jeopardize a great many jobs at home and elsewhere? Is not the safeguarding of jobs a primary ethical objective of economic life? Whatever the answers may be to such questions, Ramaer carefully points out that because of its greater impact on life, an international private enterprise has not less but more ethical responsibilities than a non-international enterprise and those additional ethical duties must be clearly formulated precisely because the massive impact of international firms on individuals across the globe is far greater than the impact of purely national enterprises.

Today, it is impossible to speak about business firms without speaking in the same breath about trade unions. The age of strictly free enterprise, the age of *laissez-faire*, is long over. Indeed, most nations located in the industrially developed parts of the globe are under governments that are as much if not more influenced by trade unions than by big business. In the United States, the coming presidential election, unlike the elections in 1972, 1968, 1960, looks more and more like a replica of the elections in 1964 and 1948, to say nothing of the elections of 1932 and 1936: a contest between big business and trade unions. It is, therefore, fortunate to have among the discussion papers a contribution by a distinguished Dutch trade-unionist, A. Hordijk, a contribution particularly relevant because of the clear-cut stand he takes. What makes his stand so clear-cut relates to his position in ethics, or rather to the position taken by the Federation of Christian Trade Unions, or CNV as it is spoken of for brevity's sake in the Netherlands. It is now, as suggested in his paper, the sole major dissenting group in the Dutch trade-unionist movement, which witnessed early this year the fusion of NKV and of NVV, that is, the Catholic and Socialist trade unions under the common name FNV. Unlike the FNV, which professes no ethical philosophy – unless sheer pragmatism is called ethical philosophy – the CNV appears to be the only trade unionist organization with an ethical philosophy, for, as Hordijk points out with great regret, the NKV seems to be shifting away from the ethical philosophy implied in the papal encyclicals.

Hordijk's paper starts with the interesting question of whether trade unions, which are a classic form of self-defense, can be a source or embodiment of ethical awareness. Is not self-defense intrinsically suspect of selfishness? Now obviously, if a trade-unionist movement like the CNV professes itself to stand on the ethics implied in the Gospels, it can become the embodiment of a truly ethical spirit. Hordijk's crucial point is – and this will undoubtedly be the source of lively arguments – that the social objectives which he derives for workers from the ethics of the Gospel, is systematically shortchanged by pragmatist trade-unionist movements, although their practical social objectives can hardly differ much from those of the CNV.

Big business logically prompts reflections on trade unionism; big business and trade unionism together prompt reflections on the process of arbitration, in a sense the topic of two papers. 'In a sense,' to be sure, because neither of the two papers deals with the question of arbitration in its primary sense, namely, with a reference to courts of arbitration. We know all too well the increasing role played by these courts in economic life. It is an open secret that the prosperity of the German Federal Republic is due in no small measure to its courts of arbitration and to the laws that govern the functioning of those courts. It is also an open secret that in the United States, the courts are functioning more and more as courts of economic arbitration. Hardly a week passes nowadays in the United States without the Supreme Court being involved in passing judgment on this or that part of the economic policy of the executive branch. The recently proposed elimination of one-tenth of those eligible for the food-stamp program has become an issue for the Supreme Court and not for Congress or for the ballot box.

While all these things are open secrets about courts of arbitration and about courts that function as if they were courts of arbitration, there is very little open discussion about the ethical principles underlying the practice of courts of arbitration. These ethical principles are tacitly assumed when in one way or another a power struggle is to be settled within the framework of society. It is in this broader sense that the ethical basis of arbitration is dealt with in Van Reijen's paper on 'Power and legitimation' and in De Wachter's paper on 'Moral policy and public policy.' In a very interesting remark Van Reijen points out that Marx's chief objection to 'bourgeois society' was that its canon of ethical norms used in business was extraneous to its economic concepts. This is, of course, true, although this does not justify Marx's contention that only such ethics of economy are ethical which are derived from economics alone or from the analysis of the tools of production. As Van Reijen points out in what seems to be the most important part of his paper, one becomes trapped in a *petitio principii* when one uses a means and legitimates or justifies the use of it at the same time from its very use. 'Legitimation,' to quote Van Reijen, 'is always transcending the simple use of something and certainly in the case of power.' Therefore, as Van Reijen concludes, 'a political system using the separation of power and legitimation of power can as such not produce rationality, this being a basis for a discussion aiming at bringing the two together. Such a system can only produce legality, not legitimation.'

The word legality leads to the very heart of De Wachter's paper on 'Moral policy and public policy.' On the face of it, legality is the direct issue in that very concrete and hotly debated issue, the question of fetal research, which De

Wachter takes, so to speak, as his case-history. Now it may appear that the legality involved in fetal research is a topic very much removed from the topic of the ethics of business decisions. Well, it may seem to be far removed, but in a very basic sense it goes to the heart of the business enterprise and for two reasons: One is that what we do with fetuses will heavily determine what kind of men or women are going to do business in the world of the future. Second, debates of fetal research, more than other debates, have brought to the forefront the question of legality versus morality, which is largely the difference that De Wachter calls public versus moral policy. The difference is not a difference between black and white, or all versus nothing. To quote De Wachter: 'The difference, in my view, is that moral policy is always about morals and nothing else, whereas public policy is about morals and many other things which definitely cannot be reduced to morals.' These are very wise words and have a great relevance to questions of business ethics. This is illustrated by a judicious remark in the Teulings' paper in which he speaks about two ways of making an ethical enterprise out of a business enterprise. One is the approach of maximizers, better known as radicals, who take one particular aspect of life, say ecology, and refuse to give consideration to any other aspect of the problem on hand. The other approach is what Teulings calls the optimisation, that is, the co-ordination of a large number of economic, ethical, and social parameters to provide the most for the largest possible number of people. Clearly, the process of optimisation is a never-ending undertaking. Its basic principle is wisdom demanding self-restraint on the part of all, and calls for a recognition of the inherent imperfection and inherent perfectibility of the human condition. This, of course, means the readiness to admit that the hour of perfect, wholly satisfactory, and final solution is a target never to be reached.

Ultimately, the question of ethics of business decisions forces upon us the decision to consider in depth the human condition. That condition is the condition of human nature, a deep topic which certainly received a treatment in depth in Stallaert's paper, 'Ethics and profit.' In his paper, Stallaert starts with the deepest philosophical questions and he does so with an impressive incisiveness. It is something like making a deep surgical incision as he cuts into the gravely sick body of modern philosophy, sick since the times of Descartes who injected into Western thought the radical distinction between objective and subjective. Since then, the objective is being reserved to the quantitative, while everything else, including ethics, is considered a purely subjective matter. This kind of distinction was very influential in bringing about the rude unethical form of capitalism which 'objectively' handled its expenditures and income, while it ignored ethics as something belonging to the 'subjective.'

Interestingly enough, this distinction forms the starting point of Schreuder's paper in which it is recalled that historically this distinction was grafted on economics by Adam Smith. He is best remembered as the author of *The Wealth of Nations* (1776), a bicentennial book in more than one sense, but he also wrote the *Theory of Moral Sentiments* (1759), a much neglected book that has little to do with questions of business. Smith's two books represent a not-at-all accidental separation of two subjects, business and ethics, and also the curious neglect which befell the latter. Until very recently this separation of business and ethics was a hallowed tenet for most theorists of economics, a tenet which received much reinforcement from Max Weber and was also defined by Karl R. Popper. Quite recently, however, the so-called normativists, as Schreuder hastens to note, revolted against the principle of value-free methodology, a principle which is ultimately based on the Cartesian dichotomy between the objective and the subjective.

As Stallaert emphasizes in his paper, the Cartesian distinction between objective and subjective is a fallacy, because even the so-called objective cannot be had without the subject, that is, the thinking, conscious individual. Stallaert's position is amply proved by modern developments in mathematics. About a hundred years ago the famous German mathematician, Krönecker, still could say that 'God created the integers and everything else was created by man.' What he meant was that in mathematics the integers represent the bedrock of objectivity and that everything else in mathematics is the subjective fancy of men. Today, mathematicians no longer entertain such illusions about integers. They are not the bedrock of objectivity. Certainly the absolute, Cartesian objectivity of mental constructs, be they quantities, ought to appear doubtful if their consistency is not self-contained, and such is indeed the case even with that arithmetic which deals with integers. As Gödel had already shown in 1931, systems of arithmetics that are non-trivial cannot have the proof of their consistency within themselves.

Whatever the need of this little extraneous support to Stallaert's starting thesis, once one accepts it, one can proceed with him without undue difficulty to his concluding thesis, namely, that ethics is a system of thought rooted in considerations about the being of man. Being the children of a Western culture until very recently steeped in Judeo-Christian tradition, we are apt to think of ethics as something given from above through the mediation of prophets and angels. Of course, one can receive a good many things from prophets and angels provided one accepts their message. At any rate, it is true even in this partly post-Christian age of ours that if a society does not believe in angels that very same society has no right to lay claim to policemen, politicians, judges, and businessmen that behave like angels. Such was my remark about five years ago at a big American university to a small group of professors who in an informal gathering deplored the rottenness of the police force in New York City, a police force then largely made up of people of Irish and Italian stock. What prompted my remark was that shortly beforehand it was argued that there was no ethics but only cultural patterns, social and tribal conditionings. If such is the case, every tribal group, whether from Brooklyn (New York) or from Breukelen (Holland), or from the West End of London or from the North Side of Chicago, can stand pat on its own 'ethics' and this will put an end to all discussions about ethics.

That such is indeed the case may best be illustrated by a story which I know from a very reliable source. The story is about the famous French general, Delattre de Tassigny, who served as a young officer in the Central African French Colonies during the late 1920's. One day he was introduced with the help of a missionary to a cannibal chief about thirty years of age who spoke impeccable French. To the inquiry of Capitain Delattre de Tassigny, the chief disclosed that as a boy he was taken to one of the port cities where a missionary befriended him. The boy, son of a cannibal chieftain, did not become a Christian, but since he was unusually intelligent, he was sent to Paris where he entered the Sorbonne. After finishing his studies, the young cannibal returned to his tribe to succeed his father as leader of the tribe. Hearing that story Capitain Delattre de Tassigny was a bit indignant. 'How can you,' he said to the cannibal chief, 'after all that education at the Sorbonne, still go on with your tribal custom of eating human flesh?' 'Ah bien sûre, mon capitain,' the chief answered, 'mais maintenant je mange avec une fourchette.' As I was told, this was the first and last time in Delattre de Tassigny's life that he could not continue a debate. Or to make the all-important application: if ethics is merely a matter of tribal custom, how could anyone debate with a Hitler, a Stalin, a Mao, the super cannibal-chieftains of our century, to say nothing of many of the smaller cannibals ravaging our culture?

Indeed, if ethics is but a tribal heritage, or social conditioning, all discussants of business ethics should discontinue their debates. They are far from doing this. Instead there is a flood of words printed about the ethics of business decisions. Part of that flood is contributed by textbooks on ethics, written by those whose philosophy renders meaningless questions about an ethics which is objectively and universally valid. Not being a businessman but a philosopher of science, my contribution to this conference had to be an analysis of the concepts of science, decision, and ethics which dominate textbooks on business decisions. Many of those textbooks deal with the mathematical tools of statistical analysis and with variational calculus applied to questions of the following type: given a certain number of variables mutually influencing one another and given a number of statistically evaluated boundary conditions, what are the procedures to follow to obtain optimum results, that is, optimum profit? A relatively few books on the science of decision-making in business deal, however, with the ethical aspects of making those decisions. I have paid special attention to two books widely used in business schools, one by R. L. Ackoff, the other by C. W. Churchman. They offer no ethics worthy of being called ethics. Their failure derives from their having adopted that shallow notion which operationalism and logical positivism provide about science. Science, when taken in its historical reality, offers not only a deeper perspective of itself than what logical positivism can provide, but also gives very valuable perspectives on the nature of decisions and on the nature of ethics. Science, as shown in my paper, 'Ethics and the science of decision-making in business: a specification of perspectives,' is an endless series of decisions, often with momentous consequences for the individual scientist's life, but also for the entire society in which he lives. Clearly, then, if science is inconceivable without readiness on the part of the individual scientist to make decisions, it is most unlikely that there can be a science of decision-making which can eliminate the agonizing part of making decisions, that is, the uncertainty inherent in decisions.

As to the perspective on ethics unfolded in my paper, it is in one basic respect in full accord with all the other papers. Such is a remarkable circumstance which deserves a little comment. The papers which formed the subject of discussion of this section of our conference were written by nine scholars of widely differing backgrounds, interests and concerns. On such a basis one would expect that their deepest wish concerning ethics in business would represent variations resembling the Gaussian curve of statistical sampling. Instead, there is hardly any distribution. There is a striking unanimity concerning the point that a definitive exposition of ethics in business cannot be had without first having a society, a global society to be sure, possessed of a substantial consensus about matters of ethics. It should seem even more encouraging that not only students of business ethics are in agreement on this point but also those deeply involved in the business enterprise itself. A good illustration of this is provided in the paper by A. Hordijk, who quotes from the proceedings of the European regional conference of the International Labour Organization held in January 1975. In its report on 'Human values in social policy' we read:

Throughout Europe we have a swelling tide of human aspirations which cut across all differences of political regime, ideological outlook, economic systems and social structure. How can we reintroduce into European societies a greater measure of freedom, a greater respect for human dignity, and a fuller measure of personal responsibility, without doing away with the minimum of discipline and order that are essential for continued stability and prosperity?

That concern for a minimum of discipline and order is the aspiration for a basic consensus in ethics. To the voice of trade unions, let me add the voice of courts concerned not with morality or ethics but with legality. The voice is that of a Chief

Justice of the United States who warned that legality cannot be maintained without a morality which is constitutive of civilization itself. The warning is all the more relevant because Earl Warren, the Chief Justice in question, was very influential in moving the United States toward the elimination of traditional ethical values from its legal system in the name of constitutional legality. But as Chief Justice Warren noted on November 12, 1962, at the Louis Marshall Award Dinner at the Jewish Theological Seminary of America in New York:

> Society would come to grief without Ethics, which is unenforceable in the Courts, and cannot be made part of Law ... Not only does Law in a civilized society presuppose ethical commitment; it presupposes the existence of a broad area of human conduct controlled only by ethical norms and not subject to Law at all ... The individual citizen may engage in practices which, on the advice of counsel, he believes strictly within the letter of the Law, but which he also knows from his own conscience are outside the bounds of propriety and the right. Thus, when he engages in such practices, he does so not at his own peril – as when he violates the Law – but at peril to the structure of civilization, involving greater stakes than any possible peril to himself ... This Law beyond the Law, as distinct from Law, is the creation of civilization and is indispensable to it ...

In the creation of a civilization, businessmen play an important part, though not the most important part. Not being a businessman, I cannot speak on their behalf, nor even articulate their innermost aspirations. But I feel certain, and the conference during which these papers were presented supports that certainty of mine, that many of them would prefer to live in a culture more unified in ethics than our modern culture is. Of our culture it is true more than of any other cultures that it is strongly based on science. The progress of science is indeed more and more the basis for the increased flourishing of business itself. It is also true of our culture that the fragmentation of its ethical beliefs received much support from a positivist interpretation of science. In this connection it is enough to think of the exploitation of Einstein's theory of relativity on behalf of the contention that everything is relative. Such is a sad development because if there is an absolutist physical theory it is Einstein's theory of general relativity. Yet, Professor Ziman, author of the book *Public Knowledge*, expressed the prevailing attitude when he wrote that although science was born in a culture steeped in a firm consensus about the rationality of nature, a firm consensus about matters of ethics would be as alien to us as a consensus about the rationality of nature was alien to the Chinese of old, who precisely because of this failed to progress to a sufficiently high level of science. Contrary to Professor Ziman, the birth of science in the Christian West presupposed a consensus not only about the rationality of science but also about ethics. If science is turning into a threat to civilization it is because we no longer possess a consensus about ethics. The same is true about business. It becomes a threat to human well-being if practiced in a cultural milieu which ridicules consensus in matters of ethics. Without that consensus we shall have no ethics worthy of that name, but only legality which is rapidly taking on an amoral character. Moreover, the consensus which is indispensable for a workable ethics is of immediate urgency for producers, consumers and marketers alike. They cannot afford the luxury of philosophers engaged in endless disputes which postpone vital decisions and commitments. Business, like life in general, is the process of making decisions. It was one of the purposes of this volume and this conference to help make business decisions to be so many contributions toward a much needed ethical consensus.

II. STANDARDS AND VALUES IN THE BUSINESS ENTERPRISE

Christiaan H. I. E. M. Teulings

1. Introduction

Ethics is a subject with a venerable history. It has been practised by curates of souls and philosophers – and, in recent times, by entrepreneurs too. That is a fact that gives pause for thought.

The schooling I had in my youth, as a layman in ethics, centered around the Ten Commandments. In that respect, the sixth commandment: 'Thou shalt not commit adultery,' was a problem because its meaning was not clear, and the seventh commandment: 'Thou shalt not steal' – a business involving thieves clambering over house fronts at night armed with masks and burglars' tools – was something for which I am simply not dextrous enough.

No wonder that for a generation brought up in this way ethics was a special subject as far removed from reality as astronomy. The fact that day-to-day life constantly confronted us with problems of good and evil was a matter which was certainly recognised in theory but not experienced as such in practice. Viewed in retrospect, the war with its inconceivable crimes against the Jews brought about a fundamental change in this attitude. Evil existed on a gigantic scale, and not only in the seamy side of society. Initially, it was a reassuring thought that others – obviously villains – had committed it. However, the post-war generation focuses attention on responsibility. Completely normal and respectable people had been involved in it or had allowed it to happen under their very noses. We too had allowed it to happen under our very noses. Anyone who had imagined that such a thing could happen only once in history, in one country, was disillusioned when in Vietnam evil once again assumed gigantic proportions. It has become evident that this can happen in a modern, extremely complex society, and that many people can be partly liable for it within an intricately entangled skein of responsibility.

Our complex society has not only brought disasters in its wake, but also an increase in material prosperity which we would have regarded as impossible thirty years ago. Now, however, this prosperity is taken for granted by those who knew things as they used to be, and certainly by the younger generation. Attention is concentrated on other things, which I should now like to label briefly as the quality of life. It has now become clear that our material prosperity also has a price: a price we pay at the expense of the quality of existence. Whether the Club of Rome is right or not, the side-effects of this industrial society are unmistakably clear to everyone. Anyone who sees growth and its side-effects ranged opposite each other – the cost which does not precede benefit but appears to follow it – starts asking questions which involve weighing the pros and cons, which concern standards and objectives. One thing which is in a state of flux is the thinking about the *raison d'être* of our institutions, and parallel with this is a new sense of morality. Some of the rules that used to be held up to us have proved to make virtually no contribution to a good human society, and perhaps accomplish the opposite. Yet there are facets of human actions which have an essential influence on the quality of all our lives but which were completely outside the Ten Commandments. Morality has emerged from the sphere of sinning behind closed doors. We are all continually confronted with moral choices with great visible effects on our fellow men.

2. The growing pluriformity of our value judgements

For almost two thousand years, our Western culture has been intimately bound up with Christianity. For a long time culture remained fairly homogeneous: the values of the West were the values of a Christian society, although there was already a discrepancy between the actions of society and the spirit of the Gospel. The social structure was homogeneous, divided into distinct compartments, and it was stable.

Even when new spiritual schools of thought arose, their values stemmed from the ancient inheritance common to us all. This is why there is a common basis in our values which must not be underestimated. By values, I mean those standards which we regard as being of the greatest importance in human existence and by which our actions can be tested. These values, which are founded in the Christian, humanist, liberal and socialist traditions can be summed up in a few key words:
– respect for the individual;
– brotherly love: do unto others as you would be done by;
– justice;
– freedom;
– responsibility: act with awareness of the consequences of your actions;
– truth and reliability.
These values themselves must be translated into action, into standards.

Standards are rules of behaviour. How do you put the values into practice? Values have a wide range of validity: they are found in various cultures, though subject to differences and changes throughout time and place.

In the process of translation into action, pluriformity grows. There is a wide margin in the common perception of good and evil. Within this margin there is scope for individual choice. The legislator has determined the lower limit of this margin more exactly in the name of society, particularly for the citizen's safety and welfare (criminal law and industrial and environmental legislation). In recent years we have observed a significant shift in standards, perhaps even in values. Pluriformity is growing side by side with change, and hence there is a margin for personal choice as well. The cause lies in the crumbling influence of the central institutions, particularly the churches, which determine standards. The result is that the legislator can only prescribe or forbid within boundaries far more limited than many would wish. The whole debate about legislation on abortion is a striking example. In addition, accents are shifting. The domain of sex used to be the principal feature of 'traditional' moral awareness. To many people, it is still the same; others have dropped the old rules without replacing them by explicit new standards. Pluriformity has grown so that governments have been compelled to withdraw to minimum positions with a broad enough basis. Hence freedom of choice increases in this domain and so does the responsibility of the individual. The sense of justice has developed in other fields and new legal obligations have therefore been formulated. This applies particularly to situations which were unknown to the old moralist and the old legislator alike, in which the quality of life is in issue (e.g. environmental legislation) or in which the individual is confronted with the institutions of this industrial society (for instance the labour laws).

Thinking on the realisation of values, on new standards – in short on ethical questions – is fed by reflection on the functioning of this society and the life of the individual in it. Questions of good and evil are not decided by majority vote, let alone by what a majority does. Unfortunately, it must be recorded that the silent majority is more inclined to listen to the voice of its own interests than to think about the realisation of values to which it still continues to subscribe, despite all its silence on the subject. Although majorities do not create standards, we still base our judgements about what is just, honest and reasonably appropriate in practice on a growing awareness of standards in the society around us. 'You can no longer do that,' is a confirmation of the validity of a postulate that was first put forward here and there by the more sensitive spirits among us. Thus, a growing awareness of standards is not a discovery of the individual, nor a referendum, but a joint learning process.

This applies to the standards which have disappeared: our fear of nudity, of mixed bathing, of attacks on the authority of parents and superiors; it also applies to new standards, for example those relating to attacks on the environment or to the caution observed in closing firms down.

3. Ethical problems are nearly always problems of choice .

In day-to-day life, it is seldom possible in practice to lay down standards in the form of rules. It is, of course, possible to formulate values and standards, but the same applies to these as to the programme of a political party: the disiderata are good and clear, but problems arise at points where values clash and lead to opposite results whenever choices have to be made. This can hardly be laid down in the form of rules, or even in priorities. Of course, we make choices of this type regularly: is it permissible for the sake of creating employment to make a product to which one objects or which must be sold by methods which cannot stand up to criticism?

Is it permissible for the sake of preserving a good atmosphere in a group to sacrifice one individual who stands in the way?

We used to be reassured that there was a difference between standards and actual behaviour. Even if we did not succeed in achieving the high standard of brotherly love in our daily lives it was nevertheless good to keep on holding it up as a shining example. Should we not become more careful in pursuing this line of thought?

The differences between teaching and living were sometimes too agonising; there was too much room for reproaches about hypocracy. These differences between standards and practice are often the result of the need to choose between two evils. Our moral system is put to the acid test when it comes to survival. Christian morality has always regarded self-defense as a valid excuse for violent or even fatal reactions; history teaches us that ample use has been made of this excuse. But the result is that standards lose their absolute validity, even if only as a rule of life here and now.

We apply them, unless . . . Unless there are no other values that oppose them. Nevertheless, we should like to apply ethical postulates against which not only the word of the law, but also our conduct can be tested.

Practical people say: 'judge my behaviour in any real choice: you can observe how I weigh standards and interests. High-sounding moral standards tell you little about the quality of my conscience.'

Christianity has constantly preached brotherly love as the all-embracing supreme value. But even this is a value that cannot be applied without weighing the pros and cons, without making a choice. A sound society cannot be built on the maximisation of self-interest – the invisible hand of Adam Smith – nor on its minimisation either. If I understand it properly, this is one of the attainments of the human sciences at the present time.

4. The gap between moralists and entrepreneurs

Entrepreneurs should not be surprised at the mistrust they encounter from moralists. For a long time they have proclaimed in every possible way that profit maximisation is their prime objective, and that this is and must be a natural need. Add to this the overwhelming influence which the large company has in society today, and it is understandable that a critical environment watches that values which were also important for our society are not disregarded. After all, the company itself says it must subordinate other values to its striving for profit – or in slightly more elegant terms, to the most rational production of goods and services possible.

As long as society's greatest needs are revealed in food and material deficiencies, a rational producer of goods meeting these deficiencies can be very useful. In the fifties, delight in progress was predominant, coupled with admiration for industry which had made such progress possible. We used the Gross National Product as a yardstick for its achievements. However, we have come to see that there are side-effects which were not or could not be evaluated in terms of money, but to which we can no longer shut our eyes. The classical standards of the company are no longer concurrent with the standards of a critical society – critical, not in the destructive sense, but in the sense of posing questions, avoiding stock answers.

But the entrepreneur, too, has his reasons for mistrust. Entrepreneurship is a matter of doing things every day, of finding rapid and specific solutions to concrete problems of working within the limits of relentless marginal conditions. Entrepreneurship means keeping a complex organisation running, and failure in this respect leads to criticism. To the entrepreneur, the moralist's questions reveal a lack of understanding of the situation, a lack of understanding of the reality of a company. The entrepreneur does not like to be bound by rules, even if he does act in accordance with them today. For tomorrow he may be faced with choices and only be able to live up to these rules at the expense of major losses elsewhere.

For anyone still unaware of this, it has now become quite clear that bribery is frowned upon by today's standards. There is every reason to adopt an internal company standard: 'We do not give bribes.' But what about the bouquet of flowers for the wife of the mayor who has an order to place, plus the case of wine for the mayor himself? What if the order is a big one and under-utilisation of capacity is a problem looming as large as life? Should you still formulate the standard and commit a minor sin now and then when it is really necessary? But the company knows the extent to which the reproach of hypocracy is ready and waiting, both externally and internally. The credibility of entrepreneurs has been too much a subject of debate to start experimenting with codes or conduct now, if there is any doubt about whether these codes can be implemented effectively under all circumstances. This applies very specifically to a company where continuity is a matter of common interest for the sake of the common value: security. Continuity is to the organisation as survival is to the individual. Standards of less importance must then sometimes be overridden. But does that end justify the means? The moralist has the answer; the entrepreneur has the problem: therein lies the gap between the two.

5. The company's changing raison d'être: towards unity of values and objectives

If the company wishes to maintain its position as one of the major institutions of our society, the gap between the reality of the company and the values of society must be bridged.

The classical company was a closed system with one simple link between it and the outside world: the market. The entrepreneur's task was to combine factors of production and his only objective was the maximisation of one yardstick: profit. In pursuing this line of thought, the objective of the company is diametrically opposed to ethics: maximisation of profit with a minimum limitation of freedom of movement by peripheral conditions of an ethical and social nature. Values in society, other than those of efficient production, are hindrances which have a strained relationship with the company's objectives. It would be exaggerated to suggest a picture in terms of then and now, as if the classical company had already disappeared and the post-industrial society were already a fact. But there has been a development in thought, both in the way things are experienced and in reality. The company in the post-industrial society is an open system, linked to the outside world through a host of relationships. Its objectives are manifold: within the context of the distribution of work in society it contributes to the prosperity of the community by producing goods and services which satisfy human needs; but at the same time it offers the people who work in it an opportunity to earn an income and to use and develop part of their abilities. It uses scarce resources – people, raw materials, capital – and must use them efficiently – i.e., profitably. It is aware that the effect of its actions extends beyond what can be evaluated in terms of money, that there are side-effects in the environment, with the consumer and elsewhere in the world.

The community is interested in all the relationships between the company and its environment; it judges the overall effect, measuring it by its entire system of values. If the company wants to continue to be an accepted institution in society, the entrepreneur's task will not only be to combine divergent factors of production but also to optimise the varying objectives of each party holding a stake in the company; then the entrepreneur will want not only to make himself responsible for the profit, but also for all the relationships with the outside world.

Ethical reflection means thinking about the question of what expectations others may have of us. If we opt for the objective of optimising all the relationships between our company and others, then ethics and the company's objectives are no longer diametrically opposed to each other on principle, even though our opinions may continue to differ about the rightness of one specific choice or another, and even though this does not bring the entrepreneur's practical problem much closer to a solution.

6. Choice is common to ethical action and economic action

The old textbooks taught us that economics is a problem of choice, a choice in the use of scarce resources. This is still the case if our objective is no longer maximisation but optimisation. Ethical problems are also problems of choice: they become problems not because of people's tendency to evil, but because of the conflicting nature of standards and interests which are valid in themselves.

The striving for the continuity of the company is certainly respectable. But it brings the company into situations which rightly merit a question mark. Is it permissible to close a given department to maintain profitability? To sell nuclear reactors to South Africa with its racial discrimination? Is is permissible to give bribes if your life depends on it? Environmental protection is all well and good, but if you do it alone it can impose a heavy burden on your cost structure and undermine your competitive position.

Anyone who subscribes to a multiple objective has to accept the fact that, in making choices, maximisation is not possible with regard to every objective. This again gives rise to conflicts with radicals, because they demand the maximum from one single viewpoint: absolute protection of the environment, absolute protection of employment. I am not saying that continuity must be given absolute preference, but that you must weigh the seriousness of the ethical objections against the importance of the need for continuity. It may involve such a high ethical value that you may be compelled to sacrifice your own continued existence, a choice which sometimes proved inescapable during the war.

At this point, I would just like to draw attention to the fact that making a choice is not only negative, choosing what not to do because you regard it as irresponsible; it is also creative, choosing what you really want within accepted margins, giving shape to a vision, to a conviction. It means choosing new forms of cooperation and new ways of contributing to prosperity and welfare.

If survival and continuity are valid arguments in weighing the ethical pros and cons, the old mistrust comes directly into its own again. Is all this not an elegant way of formulating things in order to give one's own interests a chance: if ethical action is in the company's carefully considered interests does this not still have something to do with ethics? I think it has. Every morality is a system of agreements whereby the members of a community know that they can live together with a certain degree of mutual security and protection, the protection of others and, simultaneously, of oneself. Our society would stagnate without rules. Upholding the rules and living in accordance with them is in the interests of every individual and every institution. It is essential for such a system of self-protecting standards that they should also be publicly known. With public standards, we can account for our actions openly to anyone who has a rightful interest in this respect; with public standards, everyone whose interests are at stake can ask others to account for their actions. This involves a confrontation between standards and behaviour, an explanation of the choices which have been made. One of the reasons why large companies are treated with mistrust is the great power which people see behind these gigantic organisations. It is uncontrolled power of which we have had bad experience, and uncontrolled power rapidly becomes power without standards. Accountability based on standards makes power ethically acceptable.

For some time now, the company operating for profit has been in the limelight of criticism. Companies openly admitted that material self-interest was their objective. But in essence the same applies to every organisation. Every organisation exerts a certain power, and in every organisation power threatens to corrupt those who posses it, even in the world of the non-profit organisation which is apparently motivated by idealistic objectives. There, too, action threatens to become cramped when seen from the viewpoint of one effectivity objective. Thus it makes little difference whether the aim is to win votes for a political party, members for a trade union, beds in a hospital or a number of houses in a new suburb. There, too, closed systems can arise with too little attention to other relationships with the surrounding society, too little attention to the interests of other stakeholders.

7. Who is the bearer of the standards for an organisation?

Values and standards which are implemented in practice for a group or a company bring an extra complication in their wake: in this context a company is not an operational unit. The people in the company are probably just as pluriform as society itself.

This aspect is often overlooked in theoretical considerations. People speak about the power of the multinational as though, for example, the entire thought and will of the Royal Dutch Shell were concentrated in one man. People speak about employer/employee relationships as though the old owner-entrepreneur still held sway in the large company, his income growing with every wage reduction of his workers. This pluriformity of values leads to a completely different evaluation of situations.

In the publishing business some people – generally of the older generation – have great difficulty in accepting nudity and frankness with regard to sex, although they again vary in their judgements of specific cases. For others, to help in promoting light entertainment is ethically doubtful: is it permissible to provide an opportunity for escapism in the form of diversion without any problems and thus keep people from becoming involved in serious problems? These are two different worlds of ethical sensitiveness which have no common understanding. Which of the two represents the standards of the company? What are the standards of the big modern company? Whose sense of standards decides this? It is that of the shareholders? Is it that of the supervisory board or the management? In practice the management has only limited possibilities for enforcing its sense of standards throughout the entire company.

The board of management has few ways of imposing its power if the editorial staff features more sex in a magazine's pages than was intended. It is the departmental head who determines the atmosphere of his department. This does reflect some of the values of the firm.

It is the individual official who does not observe the regulations who makes the plant stink. The management either does not know of it or cannot do much about it – after all, you cannot dismiss the departmental head because of it. What does play a part is that people in the company sense whether the management is interested in behaviour according to accepted standards. If promotion and appraisal focus on effect alone and not on other standards, this is a warning to the organisation.

In practice, the senior and middle executives probably have most influence on the company's behaviour – what Galbraith calls the technostructure.

There is a danger that only practical problems will be discussed at this level and, while the individual officials may perhaps be morally high-ranking people, the actions of the company organisation as a whole may be devoid of standards inasmuch as standards are simply left out of consideration in discussions about work. This is a great danger since the big organisation has an effect, an influence, which extends much further than the influence of the individuals.

In this connection, it is important to consider that for all the individuals in the organisation there is a complete scale of differing responsibilities. Members of the supervisory board are less directly responsible for a product or the contents of a magazine than the publisher; their responsibility is concerned more with the general spirit of the publishing house than with the individual product. The publisher is more directly responsible for the contents than the printer or the distributor, but there are limits to the printers' willingness to cooperate in everything that comes from his press. Every employee bears a share of the responsibility, in the general sense for the company's conduct; otherwise they could say: 'I will not work for a company that does that.' But the responsibility is general responsibility only and does not apply to everyone in equal measure.

In our daily work we must recognise the other person's special responsibility and give it scope, though not beyond certain limits. The same applies not only to the business enterprise, but to society as a whole as well. Indirectly, we are all working together on something we ourselves find undesirable, but there comes a point at which we refuse to take direct responsibility for something really bad. How do these overall standards come into being in a company? It is not a matter which involves top or middle management alone. In one way or another it is something which concerns the entire industrial community and it must therefore be possible to discuss it there. The works councils can play a part themselves in this process, or in guiding its course. In this way, the company in society follows two paths: its objectives are intimately bound up with the relations existing between the company and its environment; and the choices made in weighing these objectives and standards against one another are a subject of discussion in the company. Precisely because the various stakeholders have sub-objectives, this process to some extent assumes the nature of negotiation, although not all the stakeholders can find a seat at the negotiating table. The fruit of such a definition of objectives via two fields of force – one external and one internal – is part of the desired spread of, and control over, power, better than in the traditional company, but also better than in a highly centralised economy.

8. Standards as actualised values

Standards for a company are codes of conduct concerned with the relationships with all those involved both inside and outside the company – the stakeholders. For every group of stakeholders, therefore, there is a set of standards directed towards society, consumers, employees, investors, other companies, competitors and suppliers. As far as the company's conduct towards society is concerned, a great deal of attention is at present being paid to social responsibility and social audit.

One question is whether the company's responsibility is defined by government regulations or whether it has a responsibility of its own. In my view, the company does have its own responsibility for making considered choices and weighing alternatives, although the problems this involves must not be underrated. If one company is careful as regards environmental protection and its competitors are not, this may result in a cost disadvantage that can ultimately mean its downfall. That company will then sigh, 'if only the government prescribed this responsible behaviour for my competitors too, and not only nationally but internationally too ...'

Nevertheless, the government cannot judge specific cases nor prove where the limits of the unethical begin. Mental maltreatment of the subordinate escapes the eye of the legislator, as does the behaviour of the head of a family, apart from a few exceptions. Yet no one will deny that the head of a family has a moral responsibility of his own. Added to this is the fact that situations can occur in the company (for example, new production processes) which call for highly specialised knowledge in order to be able to assess the consequences. This knowledge is pre-eminently available in the company itself and this entrepreneur is therefore primarily responsible for the consequences, long before the legislator knows anything about them and can get a grip on them. As far as the consumer is concerned, is responsibility completely covered by market relationships? If the consumer buys my product is it entirely his affair? Here, too, I take the view that the producer has a responsibility of his own. Because the market is imperfect and we can, to some extent, make the consumer buy through advertising and by influencing the market. There is also the question of whether we give value for money, or whether we are not pushing products where priorities should clearly be otherwise, as, for example, selling luxury prestige goods to a poor population.

There are also products with an adverse moral effect: pornography, the arms trade, bugging devices. Opportunities offered by the market are no excuse for lack of conscience in such cases.

The critics of company-wise production also say that industry forces products on the consumer which satisfy imaginary needs. Although I see the problem, I am somewhat hesitant about the elitist aspects of such views, for who is to decide between real and imaginary needs. When the magazine *Story* was introduced it was said that a certain escapism was being forced on the consumer which kept him from satisfying his actual need for self-development. One year later 700,000 copies were being sold to 3 million readers. Who is to say that this is an unethical act on the part of the producer, and that these 3 million readers are victims because they are satisfying an imaginary need.

There is an onerous responsibility towards the employees. The manager of a company, and of a non-profit organisation as well, may be confronted with the agonising responsibilities in choosing between alternatives. He may have to choose between dismissing an entire group and the lack of continuity of employment for the others; he may have to choose for or against an employee who endangers his group, even if he knows he will break the man if his choice goes against him. These are choices for which no simple model can be given. In fact, it is a question of mutual adaptation between people and the organisation, and between people in the organisation. Adaptation has a bad name in the behavioural sciences. They say it is not the human being who should adapt to the organisation, but the organisation which must adapt to the human being. However much I applaud a shift in accent in this respect, I do not see how our social systems can function without mutual adaptation.

The company has always been an ethically functioning phenomenon. It has made choices in complex situations, for better or for worse. In fact it has also had rules for conduct at both high or low levels. In the face of the present social changes the company will not be able to go on existing without clarifying its standards and values and making them explicit. To sum up:

- Standards implicitly play a part in determining policy. The clarity of decision-making procedures and the effectiveness of policy planning are greatly encouraged by explicit standards which are known in the organisation.
- They are also necessary for motivating people. 'What kind of company do I actually work in? What is the object of my effort?' are questions which concern people today.
- It is necessary to look upon standards deriving from confrontation with the outside world as 'constraints,' of which you must clearly be aware so that you can gear your policy to them.
- In conclusion: society demands that the company, as an important social institution, act with a sense of ethical responsibility and publicly proclaim its standards, dare to defend them, and dare to let them be used as a touchstone for its actions.

III. THESES ON MAN AND PRIVATE ENTERPRISE

Johan C. Ramaer

1. On man

1.1. Man's basic ambitions, duties and rights

Man is guided by more than instinct alone; man has the capacity and therefore the responsibility of conscious and intelligent choice. He has the ambition to change and to improve. Thus, man's capacities and man's vocations are different from those of the animal – and so are his rights and duties.

Conscious and intelligent choice is only possible if freedom of thought exists, and freedom to express thoughts to fellow men. These freedoms imply man's duty to respect the exercise of such freedoms by his fellow men. The duty to respect others' freedoms implies respect for differences: in ideas and in capacities.

Man's ambition for change and improvement also implies respect for and ambition towards excellence, and recognition of the fact that those who excel lead mankind towards improvement. Excellence in leadership is one important form, especially leadership based on examples that inspire.

Man's capacity for conscious and intelligent choice and his ambition to improve has enabled him to develop and use tools on a scale that has profoundly changed the world. Because of these powers, man has a special responsibility to husband the earth's resources properly.

Man's capacity for conscious and intelligent choice has also enabled him to develop a great variety of organisations, serving a multitude of purposes. This diversity cannot exist without the freedom of association, and hence the duty to respect associations of others – including competitors.

Man's distinct properties cannot exist without a profound sense of duty in each individual in general, and in those entrusted with the responsibilities of leadership in particular. A community can only be really free if its members consciously accent such duties of their own free will. Thus, only a community of responsible people can be free. In such a community man is prepared to weigh his own needs against those of others. He is therefore prepared to compromise in cases where his own ideas and interests conflict with those of others – thereby giving others a fair chance.

Man's conditions, ideas and ambitions are multifarious; so are the forms of organisation he chooses and so – last but not least – are the compromises he should be prepared to make. But there is one principle that allows of no compromise: respect for his fellow men and his fundamental rights and duties.

The future of mankind, therefore, is not dictated by a single ideology and a single form of organisation. That would indeed be the very end of man's *raison d'être*.

2. On man's organisations

Man forms organisations to serve his interests and those of his fellow men. Man seeks cooperation because experience has taught him that organisations make possible the division of labour, so that some things can be done better by those who specialise in certain jobs. In taking part in organisations man thus acquires *scope* for improvement. But this scope cannot be acquired without sacrifice: participation in an organisation limits individual *freedoms*, as any organisation must be based on rules, a certain discipline, without which an organisation cannot function.

2.1. The state

One such organisation is the state, and one of the basic duties of the state – when founded on basic human rights – is to protect these rights for its citizens. These basic rights can be summed up as:

1. the right to *think* and to *believe*,
2. the right to *express* one's thoughts,
3. the right to *associate* and cooperate,
4. the right to *work*, to choose one's job and to make one's work available,
5. the right to *own*, privately or collectively.

In order to protect these rights for its citizens, the state has the duty to protect its territory. It also has the duty to protect the practising of the rights by its citizens. This means that the state has to enforce the laws that are made to give form and content to the rights and duties.

The state will also have to ensure that checks and balances are maintained in power relationships, both within its own structure and in society in general. Thus, the state, like its citizens, has a duty to protect the weak.

A state organisation thus conceived is called a democratic state; it maintains a system of checks and balances between executive, legislative and judicial powers. Moreover, such a state is based on the free election, by secret ballot of the legislature, with a consequent diversity of political parties which respect the outcome of the elections, and which are prepared in principle to form coalitions based on political compromises.

2.2. Private enterprise

Another form of organisation that man has created is private enterprise, which is so diversified that only its essentials can be described. These are in effect the practical application of human rights and duties to production, distribution and their social forms.

Thus, private enterprise is based on the right of enterprise. This can exist only where people feel the urge of enterprise, and where they are allowed the freedom to think and to express their thoughts, freedom of organisation, freedom to work and to choose their jobs, and to own the fruits of their work, like all others who earn from their work.

A private enterprise is an association of groups of people who make a variety of contributions, all cooperating because they have an interest in the existence of the enterprise. Employees contribute skills and work, management leadership, financiers capital, subcontractors supplies. Such groups are 'stakeholders' – they have a stake in the enterprise.

Freedom of enterprise has led to the creation of many different forms of enterprises producing a wide variety of goods and services, often competing with one another. The right to enterprise leads not only to the creation of new private enterprises, it continually inspires existing enterprises to improve existing products, to find new ones, and to change production methods and organisations.

2.3. The market

Any private enterprise is created to produce a specific product that fulfils the needs of specific customers. It communicates with these customers via the market. This is an institution that can exist only if there are potential buyers with the freedom to consume. Consumer freedom in turn can only exist if people are free to think, to express their thoughts and if they can spend money, which presupposes that they can earn it and that they can own it.

The world of man has many imperfections. But in the countries which first had private enterprise and a market economy consciously applying the fruits of science, one imperfection at least was largely eliminated: that of mass poverty, from which most of mankind has suffered throughout its history.

3. On private enterprise: its purposes and responsibilities

Organisations are formed for specific *purposes*, whether they are families, clubs, schools, political parties or enterprises. Private enterprises have two essential purposes:

Firstly, the production of goods and services that fulfil the needs of customers to such an extent that these customers feel that their total satisfaction increases when they freely exchange their money for the product supplied by the enterprise. Secondly, the earning of incomes by those who work in and for the enterprise. From these two essential purposes, the responsibilities of private enterprise can be derived:

Pursuance of the continuity of the enterprise; without continuity no organisation can function properly; continuity is a basic condition for social security.
- This means primarily that the enterprise has to attend to its customers' requirements;
- Secondly, it means that those who bear management responsibility must ensure that the various stakeholders in the enterprise get a fair share of the income, so that each of them continues to contribute his share to the total effort of the enterprise. Moreover the managers will have to ensure that sufficient means are available to ensure future continuity and growth.

An enterprise has the obligation to bring forth more value than it uses, especially in a world with exhaustible resources. This means that a profit has to be earned. Thus, profit is an essential yardstick for success. At the same time profit is at the root of the creation of new capital for new productive capacity and for new wealth and future well-being.

The responsibility of the enterprise to bring forth more value than it uses also applies to immaterial values, and especially the capabilities and other qualities of its employees. This is in the interests of the employees and also of the enterprise, as it cannot remain competitive without developing all its assets.

Another responsibility of private enterprise is to ensure that the same basic rights to which it owes its existence are respected within the community of the enterprise. Like any individual, an organisation of people such as a private enterprise has the responsibility to take into account the effects of its intended operations on the society around it.

Thus, an enterprise must communicate with its environment, not only with its customers via the market mechanism, but also with other groups affected by it via other channels of communication. Relevant questions include the environment, indirect effects of its activities, the use of scarce resources, the health and security of citizens.

Last but not least, it is the task of those with managerial responsibility in the enterprise to weigh the above responsibilities and to take decisions in accordance with the moral standards generally accepted in the society of which the enterprise forms part.

4. On international private enterprise

Private enterprises operating internationally bear the same responsibilities as private enterprises operating in one country. But the international dimension creates certain additional responsibilities. In their conduct of affairs, international companies should respect the differences in cultures, laws, moral standards and customs as between the countries in which they operate, thereby enabling the managements of their national companies to be loyal citizens of their countries of establishment. This also implies a careful and fair weighing of emergent international and national standards wherever these might conflict. The organisation of international companies must therefore allow managements in individual countries the necessary scope to integrate their company into the national socio-economic structure. This means that the national company managements must have a considerable degree of autonomy, especially in regard to industrial relations.

The previous point presupposes a process of decision-preparation and decision-making based on mutual respect and consent between the staff departments and managements of the parent company and national companies. Mutual respect and consent cannot exist if there is no common ground in the form of certain values considered to be worth pursuing. This is essential for any organisation, but in a world-wide organisation the common ground is inevitably more dynamic and diversified, owing to the wide international differences in culture. Such common ground has to be developed by many years of communication between people from different countries.

IV. A MORAL INTERREGNUM FOR MULTINATIONALS IN THE THIRD WORLD?

Pjotr Hesseling

In the past twenty years the multinational enterprise has received considerable attention, as if it were an entity with special rights and obligations, I will not attempt to summarize the extensive literature but will instead refer to a recent bibliography (Brooke, 1977). The 10,000 or more (large) enterprises reported by the European Commission to have two or more foreign subsidiaries (Euser, 1977, p. 8) and the unknown number of smaller or temporary business concerns operating in a guest country from a foreign base have a great variety of goals and operations. The scanty evidence on actual practices does not yet permit any generalization, for instance, based on a few reported examples of amoral behaviour. I shall confine my considerations to the question of whether the impact of multinationals upon developing countries necessitates special moral rights and obligations. As regards this, my assumption is that the balance between interest and power on the one hand and societal responsibility for a subtle development process on the other can easily be disturbed. Business ethics seem to be required especially in the relationships between rich and poor, mighty and powerless, established nation states with their own codes of conduct and new nation states where traditional rights and obligations have not yet been translated into terms of modern business.

There has been long-term interest in the moral legitimacy of business. As Schreuder points out (this volume), Adam Smith, one of the founders of the science of economics, started as a moral philosopher and his *Theory of the moral sentiments* (1759) should be related to his *Wealth of Nations* (1776). However, moral discussions on the nature and causes of the wealth of nations appear to be more applicable to power relationships between the wealthy than between the wealthy and the needy.

1. The nature of formal organizations

There are two levels of discussion. Firstly, a general level relating to codes of conduct for multinationals as adopted or recommended by international agencies such as the UN, OECD and EEC. Various codes of conduct are at present in the process of being reconsidered also by advisory and voluntary associations including the International Chamber of Commerce (Guidelines for International Investment, adopted by the Council on 29, November 1972), the Business and Industry Advisory Committee to the OECD (Commentary of June 22, 1976) and many discussions in national management associations preparatory to the world congress of the CIOS (Comité International d'Organisation Scientifique) in Bombay in 1978 where an international code of conduct for management will be a central theme.

At this level the main concern seems to be an international agreement on general policies, disclosure of information, competition, financing, taxation, employment and industrial relations, and science and technology (following the OECD recommendations of June 1976): 'The guidelines are not aimed at introducing differences of treatment between multinational and domestic enterprises; wherever relevant they reflect good practice for all' (Annex, No. 9), and 'Observance of the guidelines is voluntary and not legally enforceable' (Annex, No. 6). In this sense the many noble intentions assume equal opportunities and stress mutual confidence and harmony. The starting point seems to be a balanced international business community and there is no special adaptation to developing countries. One of the real problems of development seems to be where the endogenous balance between natural environment, social relations, education, production, consumption and well-being is not yet attained and where representatives of the international community implant foreign patterns of industry and business. In such a confrontation international business as a whole has 'the responsibility of guaranteeing the conditions for the self-reliant development of each society' (see 'And what now? The 1973 Dag Hammarskjöld Report on Development and International Cooperation,' 1973). However, such general considerations and noble intentions are difficult to translate for an individual company, unless other companies agree on similar guidelines or long-term investment might be better protected than without such guarantees. If officials of an international company agreed, for instance, that advanced electronic equipment would not fit in with the endogenous development of a particular country and encourage the adaptation of technology, while competitors preferred to provide the most advanced technology even if proper requirements for the educational infrastructure did not seem to be met, business practice could not in such a case be expected to guarantee balanced development. This would suggest that the nature of international business does not fit the development process in the Third World or, to follow Jaki's reasoning (this volume), that decision-making in business might be amoral.

A recent discussion related to an international banking enterprise which had been publicly attacked because of its investments in the Republic of South Africa. After long discussions and a partial boycott, the investment policy was changed. According to one party concerned, the change reflected moral considerations, but according to another, it reflected a different balance between major customers who opposed the policy and would withdraw their money and the actual size and prospects of the South African business. At the pragmatic level it seems difficult to discover the real reason for the change in policy. Even if one or more of the company's officials accepted moral considerations for changing the policy, the final decision by the board might reflect a rational decision regarding the balance between customer and public relations. In the long run it even seems difficult to assess whether the withdrawal from South Africa would promote more balanced development.

In another recent debate on the role of multinationals in a new international order at the European Centre for Study and Information on Multinational Corporations (ECSIM) on 18, November 1976 in Brussels, a powerful group from nine European countries responded to the ideas of J. Tinbergen, co-ordinator of the Third Report to the Club of Rome, entitled 'Reshaping the International Order' (1976). It was argued that transnational enterprises have been very instrumental in increasing production and developing technology. The gap in capital investment between Western Europe and developing countries is very wide (some figures range from 4,000 to 10,000 dollars per employee in Western Europe, whereas developing countries have at most about 1,000 dollars per employee). The R.I.O. report strongly recommends some sort of countervailing power to bridge the existing gap and stimulate new codes of conduct. In the discussion it became clear that a moral obligation to help the developing countries can only be accepted if it is good business. Self-interest is the only motive for action (p. 23). As Adam Smith wrote: 'it is not from the benevolence of the butcher, the brewer, or the baker, that we expect our dinner, but from their regard for their own interest.' Instead of Adam Smith's 'invisible hand' one looks for a truly international code of conduct applicable to multinational companies and governments. Fundamentally, it seems very difficult for large formal organizations such as business enterprises to claim and express moral obligations. To quote P. M. Blau:

Formal organization makes power liquid by transforming the potential power of financial resources, which are inherently liquid, into actual power over employees dependent on their incomes, and by vesting this power in the form of institutionalized (impersonal) authority in official positions. Since both financial resources and official authority reside in the formal organization and do not belong to its particular members, the powers emanating from them can readily be transferred from existing personnel to new replacements and from one position to another ... Thus, organizational power can be accumulated in very large amounts as well as transferred, which makes it much more liquid than personal power (Blau, 1974, 19–20).

Even if top executives have strong moral beliefs, the nature of formal organizations shields them from surveillance and control in actual practice. It is possible to replace sensitive and ethical office holders during a critical stage in the operation of a subsidiary by more ruthless office holders, if it would suit the particular climate of the host country.

To sum this up, at the general level of impersonal power vested in formal organizations which struggle for survival in a competitive pragmatic world of international business – only the countervailing power of government, trade unions, consumer organizations and professional associations is a guarantee of moral conduct by international business. Any effort to establish new codes of conduct for multinational corporations is welcome but their impact is dependent on enforceable rules and laws. Because many developing countries have dual moral standards – one traditional within the family and groups of origin and one implanted by the international business community without a countervailing infrastructure – they need special protection against direct confrontation with foreign subsidiaries. The nature of formal organizations does not provide any such shelter.

2. Personal responsibility

The second level of discussion is that of personal responsibility. In contrast to the earlier ethos of individual work and effort, which required industry, sobriety, thrift, punctuality, and postponement of early reward, based upon a Calvinistic, puritan religion, there is a new hedonistic and materialist culture where individuals unashamedly grasp for self-enrichment. At this level, the discussion is very fluid. Many examples from developing countries could provide the material for a new theory of conspicuous consumption by the new leisure class, as Thorstein Veblen wrote about the United States in 1899. But here again the moral issue is not so simple. If traditional customs require, for instance, a splendid display of wealth in order to repay debts to the community, dualistic economic development might show a transition from traditional to modern behaviour. A curious example is the 'potlatch' of the American Indians of the northwest coast, in which a successful Kwakiutl invites all his friends and neighbours to a feast (a potlatch) at which he gives away all the accumulated results of long years of labour. In its original context the 'potlatch' was the linchpin of the entire social system. 'It redistributed food and wealth. It validated changes in social status. It converted the wealth given by the host into prestige for the host and provided the motivation for keeping up the cycle of exchanges' (E. E. Le Clair and H. K. Schneider, 1968, p. 296).

However, if we collect anthropological evidence from all over the world (including the West), we find so many variations in culture and social conditions that each type of behaviour, however amoral it may seem, can be explained by some traditional pattern. As Jaki rightly remarks: 'this will put an end to all discussions about ethics.'

Bribery then becomes an accepted way of exchanging favours, nepotism an accepted way of selecting officers and so on. If we accept subjective culture as the basis of behaviour, as Triandis (1972) did, for instance, we can find inductive, data-related evidence for various behaviour patterns, also in inter-cultural groups, but we cannot cope with the moral issues. A more promising approach to personal responsibility is the distinction between 'minimum' and 'maximum man', as presented by Zaleznik and Kets de Vries (1975). They use it to describe two antithetical styles of leadership, consensus and charismatic. The minimum man is the effective negotiator, able to listen to various points of view, highly rational and pragmatic, understanding the nature of trade-offs, bargains and the distribution of rewards. Decisions are, at their best, equitably balanced between the needs of the different constituents and the objective demands of production, technology, and hard economics. They claim that the highly ritualized approach of Japanese leaders is an extreme example of this consensus style (Zaleznik and De Vries, 1975, pp. 232–233). Ethical questions are rarely acknowledged. He is constantly scanning with his radar for opinions and sources of power in others, tending by the very structure of his personality not to have an integrated set of commitments, and he prefers the pragmatic, self-serving choice, ethical or not (p. 252). Hardly surprisingly, they take Richard Nixon as an example. The maximum man on the other hand is a charismatic leader, a great innovator with an extremely high self-esteem. He carries within his psyche a stable audience as a reference point for judgment. He is independent, inner-directed and constantly finds opportunities to make large-scale ethical or unethical decisions (pp. 241, 242, 252). Besides the examples of De Gaulle and Hitler, they describe the case of a Texas businessman who got money on collateral for grain elevators that simply did not exist. But he was a fundamentalist in his religions beliefs and had, for example, separate swimming pools for men and women (p. 253).

In contrast to the unethical actions of maximum men, which are often gross and unambiguous, the ethics of the minimum man and consensus are subtle and difficult to pin down. The maximum man behaves unethically because he believes that *he* is right and justified; the minimum man performs unethical acts in the name of institutional narcissisms: the corporation can do no wrong (pp. 253–254).

In their final analysis on philosophers and kings they blame the new corporate culture where the former richness in the culture of institutions that provided material for deepening personal experience has been depleted by the pro-gramming of power. Despite the many fascinating case studies of leadership and examples of refreshing analysis I doubt whether this dichotomy between minimum and maximum man – or other-directed and inner-directed types, as David Riesman labelled them in *The lonely crowd* (1950) – is satisfactory for coping with moral issues such as the impact of multinationals upon developing countries. If the corporate representative were a minimum man, he would try to strike a balance between public relations and hard economics: if bribery is an accepted way of doing business, then he will bribe; if hard selling is profitable, then he will do it, and so on. No proper standard of ethical behaviour seems to be independent but only a pragmatic trade-off in negotiations. If a maximum man were selected as a corporate representative in developing countries it would depend on his own internal image of right or wrong without any other frame of reference. The only answer might be individual biography but this is a difficult approach for a new corporate ethos in coping with the Third World.

3. The need for an intermediate level of business ethos

The search for a new corporate ethos which might respect and stimulate endogenous development in the Third World has come to a deadlock. At the general level it depends on a new political power that can enforce a code of conduct from multinational corporations and governments. However, a global authority does not yet exist and there is no agreement on a fair international division of labour, wealth and knowledge. Of course, we can express the desirability of such a new order and support any move in the 'right' direction, but in the meantime the gap between the present level of the developing countries and that of the advanced countries is widening. The interregnum between a new international order, however utopian, and the present imbalance of power and wealth needs to be bridged without reference to a real international authority.

At the personal level we can only refer to the cultures of origin. In Western development the traditional emphasis on a common religion or religious ethos has been replaced by an ethical pluralism with a strong pragmatic inclination. I agree with Levitt (1976) that the basic appeal of today's anti-business ideology is moral and not economic or political. The appeal of 'various collectivistic, socialistic, and communitarian communistic economic arrangements ... is indifferent to their functionality' (p. 3). There is a widening gap between effective and efficient allocation of scarce resources where science can be instrumental in designing alternative solutions on the one hand and moral issues of equality, fairness and human goals of self-reliance and self-development on the other. Any doubt about the moral legitimacy of business will be met with arguments on functional effectiveness in relation to the operational infirmities in socialistic and collectivistic economies. But moral arguments cannot be refuted with pragmatic evidence. It does not seem fair to blame the multinationals, because they represent our business ideology and have been instrumental in our material welfare. I do not know of any alternative ethical regime that has proved to be equally successful in operational effectiveness and can be transferred at a global level.

The case of Japan has been frequently referred to: 'The rate of development in Japan has been about twice as high as in most other countries, if not higher. What is happening, or has already happened in Japan, can therefore be regarded as a fast-motion movie of the kinds of things that might happen in other parts of the world' (Tinbergen, 1976, p. 16). The basis of moral obligations of Japanese business towards developing countries does not lead to a new ethos at a personal or general level. The Japanese concepts of *on* and *giri* (moral rights and obligations) derive from a division between an inner world (*nai* or *uchi*) and an outer world (*gai* or *soto*). In the proper inner world of the community of origin there are natural human feelings (*ninjo*) which stimulate human development, and with a subtle set of mutual exchanges it is possible to create similar conditions outside the direct environment; but for the real outside world, as in developing countries, 'one loses his shame or leaves his shame at home' as a Japanese proverb says.

It is of course impossible to describe the Japanese concepts of moral obligations and rights in more detail, but I would stress that each ethical code of conduct seems to develop within an inner circle where sanctions become internalized. The basic operation seems to be how to extend moral rights and obligations towards 'outsiders' who do not share our way of life.

4. The development gap

The confrontation between multinationals, as representatives of our advanced technical and economic development, and industrial efforts in developing countries reflects one of the major concerns of our time. Multinationals are based on universal and global rationality in allocating resources. They have been successful in designing work processes for their particular product-range which are highly effective and efficient and utilize research and development for continuous improvement of products and processes. They tend to show a high degree of utilization of capital and knowledge. Most multinationals investing in developing countries transfer their know-how without adaptation to the Third World (Reuber, 1973). The codes of conduct underlying these work processes are implicit and emphasize rationality, time-consciousness, task-oriented behaviour, performance, skill and knowledge. Moral rights and obligations are not particularly developed unless they are work-related. To quote Arnold Toynbee in a discussion with D. Ikeda: 'power conferred by technology has recently increased to an unprecedented degree at an unprecedented rate, while the average level of the moral – or immoral – behaviour of the human being who now wield this vastly increased power has remained stationary, or may actually have declined' (Toynbee and Ikeda, 1976). The multinationals may be instrumental agencies in transferring know-how but not the underlying codes of conduct.

Developing countries, in all their variations, are in a difficult and subtle process of re-orientation from their own cultures of origin. There might be valuable cores of traditional craftmanship with strict moral rights and obligations but often there is also an informal urban sector (Breman, 1976) where a great variety of irregular, 'self-employed' people try to earn a hard living by odd jobs outside the traditional protection of their village. The presence of a multinational subsidiary obviously has tremendous attraction, but anybody succeeding in being selected as an employee is confronted with a gap between the traditional and informal sectors on the one hand and the modern sector on the other. A dualistic economy seems to require a dualistic code of conduct. Even more than dualistic, because development assumes not only the transition from a traditional to a modern economy but, perhaps even more difficult, a transition from informal urban patterns to more formal standards of work. There is no simple answer to this dichotomy between a global multinational culture with advanced technology and a state of development with traditional and informal urban sectors. It is necessary, but not sufficient, to rely on a personal code of conduct adopted by representatives of multinationals in the Third World. An international agreement on codes of conduct would be important, but without sanctions it cannot be very effective.

5. Some proposals

My own suggestion would be to develop an intermediate level of moral obligations and rights between multinationals and developing countries, with special emphasis on local needs and on narrowing the gap in power, knowledge and welfare.

Firstly, it would be important to select, train and evaluate representatives of multinationals in such a way that they are not only effective in their direct operations but are ready to transfer their knowledge and skills to their local counterparts. Moreover, they should respect and understand the particular development process with its critical dimensions. For example, it is not enough to pay equal, or usually better salaries than local industry to their exployees but also to avoid splendid isolation within the immediate environment. The expatriate managers' style of living should also be adapted to local conditions. The traditional relationship between master and servant for instance, might include not only the economic dimension but also the responsibility for family and education for which a higher salary is no substitute. It is impossible to prescribe conduct in detail. Every foreign community usually has a long list of anecdotes but it is rarely checked with local insiders.

Secondly, it would be important to demand a high moral standard from representatives in order to guarantee that their knowledge, skill and effort are applied for the poorer and weaker in the host country. But this requirement is not very operational unless it can be specified. This does not imply leniency, but rather sincere interest in development processes. Nor is it a measurable attitude expressing noble aspirations for helping the poor, but indicates more fundamental integrity and wisdom. Such a moral standard is personal and internalized but can be supported by a home base or a reference group. It cannot be enforced by an international code of conduct, for instance, but can only be stimulated.

The danger of this second requirement of a high moral standard, which cannot be operationalized in the same way as legal obligations and standards of functional performance, might be that it leads to a vague 'ethical reveille' and 'law and order.' The 'ethical reveille' which was used for example in the Dutch elections of 1977 seems to attract many people who grumble about the increase in crime, abuses of social security, changes in sexual attitudes and in general about divergences from one's own preferred way of life. It can be used unspecified as a weapon against a pluriform, many-sided development. The 'law and order' symptom is very familiar both in advanced and developing countries as a reaction to change. As general terms, 'high moral standard,' 'ethical reveille,' 'law and order' are harmful rather than helpful in preventing an unbalanced impact by multinationals on developing countries. A practical solution for developing a high moral standard between representatives of multinationals and their counterparts in developing countries is an integrated set of operational procedures.

These procedures include:

1. Any contract between multinationals and developing countries on products, production processes or services should specify not only functional requirements such as price, quality and quantity but also complementary codes of conduct from both sides. These complementary codes of conduct might be related to government agencies, trade unions or representatives of the local community. In the advanced countries, the function of accounting, for example, 'is still oriented towards the fallacy of misplaced correctness – the historical evidence – and narrow purposes... We tend to disregard what cannot be measured 'objectively'... The developing nations will face the problems ... where the accounting function demands extension to societal measurement rather than to purely enterprise measurement' (Enthoven, 1973, pp. 17-3, 17-4).

   There is increasing awareness of a new type of social auditor who can bridge the credibility gap between business enterprises and socio-economic development. This new function should be specified by the host country and by the multinationals. There is no need to wait until general global agreement has been reached. Experiments for particular projects are required and only evaluation of the outcome will suggest new developments.

2. Formal education and training for managers and administrators should include ethical considerations. It is a pity that recent surveys of management and administrative education and training, such as those by Mailick (1974) and Taylor (1975), emphasize methods and techniques rather than codes of conduct. Many educators and trainers such as R. Revans (in Mailick) personally emphasize the process of internalization of behavioural norms but explicit treatment of ethical considerations in management is rare, anecdotal and off the main stream. A mutual basis of trust between managers, as caretakers of welfare and employment, and local representatives of communities, the labour force and consumers is needed. Research into management needs must be based on concern for local customs and the practical implications in preference to extrapolating Western patterns and know-how (Morello, 1972). Without a moralistic attitude, as if Western history had shown a higher, teachable level of morality, education and training must cope with moral issues as an essential issue. In the Dutch university system, for example, three objectives are recognized: education, research and develop-

ment for responsible citizenship. Mass education and advanced research do not add emphasis to this third objective of societal responsibility. Smaller residential colleges with personal relationships are better alternatives than many present-day mass universities.

3. Regular meetings between managers of multinational companies and representatives of local communities at the regional level could provide a platform for ethical and other cultural issues. To complement technical-economic meetings, it is important to stimulate smaller and rather informal meetings at which critical issues related to the confrontation between multinationals and local industry and the community can be freely discussed. These issues might include differences in salary and style of living as between expatriates and local managers, the prejudices on both sides, corruption, nepotism or abuse of power. Even without factual evidence, rumours, misunderstanding and distrust create an explosive climate. Since ethical questions (not directly illegal but relating to the 'right' utilization of power and money) permeate business practises, open discussion might help to create the climate of trust and personal credibility which is the basis for any human transaction. A useful example of the type of meeting was, to my mind, the first regional seminar on business and culture in South and Southeast Asia (Jakarta, 1976), where underlying issues were more important than management methods as a box of useful instruments.

4. As a last suggestion, it is essential to cope with the availability and utilization of data and intelligence collected by the multinational companies or other representatives of the advanced countries. Since *The rise and fall of project Camelot* (Horowitz, 1967), there has been an increasing awareness of the lack of accessibility by developing countries to data on their own material and human resources collected by foreigners. Frequently, the data can only be interpreted with the help of specialized agencies at the headquarters, and local research capacity within government is underdeveloped. Elsewhere I have written with D. Graves:

The danger of scientific colonialism looms large in cross-cultural studies, because the centre of gravity for the acquisition of knowledge about national (organizational) behaviour tends to be located outside the nation itself . . . It is understandable that governments are suspicious about (organization) research where national researchers are used only as go-betweens or data collectors on behalf of a research centre abroad . . . (Graves, 1973, p. 327).

In the Dutch government policy formulated in Bilateral Development Cooperation (1976), J. P. Pronk rightly emphasized the need for local research capacity. Unfortunately, the conditions for continuous research cooperation are not yet favourable. In the future there will be a moral obligation to establish a research partnership in order to share available information.

6. Conclusions

This reflection on the nature of the confrontation between multinationals and developing countries does not suggest that representatives of multinationals should be made the scapegoats for unbalanced growth. It has become clear that moral rights and obligations prevade business transactions. It is not sufficient to emphasize functional requirements for cooperation and transfer: Management and organization cannot be reduced to knowledge and skills but are based on moral integrity and trust between the constituents. The body of knowledge and skills should be complemented by codes of conduct and the right behaviour. An intermediate set of practical requirements is suggested in between an universal level and personal responsibility. This interrelated set calls for a reorientation of management training, education and research, which should include ethical considerations for partnership and equal opportunities. This is not a plea for a moralistic attitude but, rather, concern for the subtle and special situations in a development process. Nor is it limited to an idealistic image of noble intentions, but rather relates to the practical implications of the appropriate and right level of management within each country. I agree with Ramaer (this volume) that there might be universal theses on man and private enterprise but would like to stress that there are unequal opportunities and urgent needs in developing countries which call for special consideration.

References

And what now? The 1973 Dag Hammarskjöld Report on Development and International Co-operation, 1973, *Development Dialogue* No. $\frac{1}{2}$, Uppsala.
Blau, P. M., 1974, *On the nature of organizations*, New York: Wiley.
Breman, J. 1976, *Een dualistisch arbeidsstelsel*, Rotterdam: Van Gennep.
Brooke, M. Z., M. Black and P. Neville, editors, 1977, *Bibliography of international business*. London: Macmillan.
Business and Industry Advisory Committee to O.E.C.D., 1976, *Commentary on guidelines for multinational enterprises*, Paris.
Enthoven, A. J. H., 1973, *Accounting and economic development*, Ph.D. thesis, Rotterdam.
Euser, B. G., 1977, 'Multinationaal ondernemen – strategisch interregnum', in *Tijdschrift voor Ondernemingsrecht*, 1, 7–14.
Graves, D., editor, 1973, *Management research: a cross-cultural perspective*, Amsterdam: Elsevier.
Horowitz, I. L., 1967, *The rise and fall of project Camelot*, Massachusetts.
LeClair, E. E. and H. K. Schneider, editors, 1968, *Economic Anthropology*, New York: Holt.

Levitt, Th., 1976, *The moral basis of business*, Utrecht: Berenschot.

Mailick, S., editor, 1974, *The making of the manager*, New York: Doubleday.

Morello, G., editor, 1972, *Management development for industrializing countries*, Wiesbaden: Gabler.

Reuber, G. L., 1973, *Private foreign investment in development*, Clarendon Press.

Riesman, D., 1950, *The lonely crowd*, New York: Yale University Press.

Smith, Adam, 1973, *An inquiry into the nature and causes of the wealth of nations* (or. 1776) edition Masterworks of Economics, vol. 1, New York: McGraw-Hill.

Taylor, B. and G. L. Lippitt, editors, 1975, *Management development and training handbook*, London: McGraw-Hill.

Tinbergen, J., 1976, *The role of multinationals in a new international order*, a debate at the European Centre for Study and Information on Multinational corporations (ECSIM), Brussels.

Tinbergen, J., 1976, *Reshaping the international order*. New York: Dutton.

Toynbee, Arnold, and Daisaku Ikeda, 1976, *Choosing life, a dialogue*, London: Oxford University Press.

Triandis, H. C., 1972, *The analysis of subjective culture*. New York: Wiley.

Veblen, Th., 1953, *The theory of the leisure class* (or. 1899), ed. New York: Mentor.

Zaleznik, A. and M. F. R. Kets de Vries, 1975, *Power and the corporate mind*. Boston: Houghton.

V. TRADE UNIONISM AND ETHICS

Arij Hordijk

1. Introduction

Surprisingly perhaps, this introduction attempts to show that trade unionism is concerned with ethical attitudes and values. Many people consider trade unions necessary as a countervailing force against the power of the employers. For this reason alone, it might seem somewhat ludicrous to link ethics (teaching us how to deal with one another as human beings) with trade union activities.

In a society in which all groups seek to defend their own interests to the fullest possible extent, it is difficult to believe that an interest group like a trade union can furnish us with a code of ethics. Trade unions are commonly believed to think and act primarily in terms of power and struggle and to have little to do with ethical issues. In everyday life we are faced with the fact that any self-respecting trade union has to fight against an undue concentration of power in the hands of management. Therefore it is often said – and to some extent rightly said – that a trade union should first of all think in terms of bread and butter, of material interests, higher wages and better working conditions. We encounter a similar problem in discussing whether or not an enterprise should have an ethical code of conduct. More specifically, one might ask: 'Is management obliged to take ethical values into account in achieving or (re-)formulating the objectives of the firm?'

Whether we like it or not, questions such as these are becoming increasingly important. Despite a relatively high standard of living in the Western world, there is a growing feeling of dissatisfaction. This is the very reason why we see so many efforts to make society more human, freer, more responsible and more dignified. It is hardly surprising that voices are being raised in favour of introducing socio-ethical norms and values in discussing the need for a society with human dignity at its pivot.

Very few people would nowadays deny that in some way or other we should integrate ethical options in both managerial and trade union policies. Differences arise, however, when we wonder how we should introduce these options into practical social policy and social responsibility. At the European regional conference of the International Labour Organization at the beginning of January 1975, there was a full debate on a report entitled 'Human Values in Social Policy.' One passage in the report reads:

Throughout Europe we have a swelling tide of human aspirations which cut across all differences of political régime, ideological outlook, economic system and social structure. How can we reintroduce into European societies a greater measure of freedom, a greater respect for human dignity, and a fuller measure of personal responsibility, without doing away with the minimum of discipline and order that are essential for continued stability and prosperity?

This quotation makes it quite clear that economic and socio-ethical aspects require an integral approach. Moreover, we should not forget that there is a close connection between events in society at large and events in the business world. Employers and employees, and their respective organizations, have to respond to a challenge aimed at restructuring our society in more human terms. They should be aware of the fact that our standard of living pertains to both the welfare and well-being of mankind.

2. Individualism or collectivism?

There is no neutral approach to ethics. Both in personal and social ethics we are guided by philosophical or religious views. Terms such as freedom, responsibility, power cannot be used without attaching value to them. One's religious and philosophical conviction is decisive for the way in which one wants to introduce or implement improvements in society, including improvements in the modern industrial enterprise. It is impossible to eliminate presuppositions because everyone has a certain view of the world and of life. Most people will agree with this. Difficulties arise the moment ethical options have to be translated into concrete aims and objectives.

In business life we are frequently confronted with the view that we should stick to our personal ethical opinions only. Introducing ethical issues in decision or policy-making processes is considered dangerous and contrary to a neutral, objective approach. Ever since the philosophy of rationalism was accepted as a substitute for religion, we have been confronted with the one-sided idea that our problems can be solved by purely scientific means, freed from all transcendent values. The notion of 'scientific management' was commonly accepted as the only objective way in which the modern enterprise could be run. It is hardly surprising, therefore, that our current industrial relations system is in such a state of crisis.

Many critics of our 'capitalist society' mistrust the interest shown by management in humanizing work and working conditions. They suspect that a change of heart by management is motivated by the expectation that this new approach will yield bigger profits. It is important to note that the renewed interest in the Marxist option does not necessarily reflect a new interest in Marx's economic theories or scientific socialism. Rather, it indicates a new concern for the ethical approach which gives full respect to human dignity.

In Marxist philosophy we are faced with the belief that the freedom and responsibility of mankind are basically safeguarded by collectivism, by man in community. Private enterprise must be replaced by state enterprise. Experience in Eastern Europe shows that this has almost always merely meant a shift in power. The so-called worker-owned or nationally-owned enterprises, however, are in fact based on the same exigencies as enterprises in the West. The nature of the modern enterprise has remained the same. The main difference is, the Marxists say, that freedom and responsibility can be safeguarded better by a system of collectivism. Many people say that the renewed interest in ideological discussion means that management and trade unions will have to steer a middle course between the Scylla of neo-capitalism and the Charybdis of collectivism. But, the question is: does this mean that the only way out is a balance of power between these two entities? The notion of countervailing power presented by John Kenneth Galbraith is significant in this respect. Many employers' and workers' representatives regard this notion as a real means of equalizing the powers that meet inside or outside the enterprise. This poses the question of whether it is possible to establish equilibrium between management control and workers' control. The gap between individual and social ethics has been reduced to the discussion of whether we opt for individualism or collectivism.

3. The Christian-social idea

In our time it is becoming more and more evident that the shaping of society depends on views about the world and about life. There is an unmistakable resistance to the domination of technology and hence to the rationalistic and pragmatic solutions that are often suggested. The call for the establishment of a counter-culture is in fact the refusal of people to acquiesce in a world in which technology, economic growth, commercial manipulation etc., have become so dominant that basic human needs can hardly be fulfilled.

Mankind is on the move and finds itself in a period of rapid transition both materially and spiritually. We are in a period of fundamental reorientation. There is a tendency to do away with (ethical) philosophical ideas stemming from

Enlightenment and Utilitarianism. These brain-children of Rationalism are gradually being replaced by irrational, transcendental approaches and attitudes. The medieval mystic Eckhart, and a number of Eastern religions are receiving more attention than ever before.

In the trade union movement – nationally and internationally – we observe a desire to give the workers more than good material conditions alone. Generally speaking, it can be said that the trade union movement is trying to guide social-economic development for the benefit of the workers. Notions of human dignity, social justice, solidarity, freedom, righteousness, play an important part in discussions on the trade unions aims. Using Dr. W. Albeda's terminology, we can say that the issue in the trade union movement is that of giving the worker his rightful position as a producer and a free human being in society (cf. De Rol van de Vakbeweging).

In the Federation of Christian Trade Unions' programme, published in 1970, we read the following about its social philosophy:

... the Federation believes that man was created to be free. At the same time he has a responsibility to God and his fellow-men. It believes that acceptance of and faith in these basic ideas are of the utmost importance in our attempts to build a society in which man can exist and live in conformity with his Creator's intentions.

At the beginning of the Federation's regulations there are similar formulations: for instance:

In establishing and carrying out its policy and course of action the Federation seeks the guidance of the liberating power of the Gospel. The Christian trade union movement is aware that the message of the Gospel is not limited to individuals. It also contains norms for relationships between peoples ...

The fundamental choice of a responsible society does not coincide with the view that conflicting interests of employers and workers are irreconcilable and that they can only be settled by means of a struggle for power. To take conflicting claims and positions of power as our starting point would deny our collective responsibility and the common task of employers and workers to bridge contrasting interests on the basis of justice and neighbourly love. For this reason the Federation firmly rejects the doctrine and practice of the class struggle in any form whatsoever.

In conclusion, the Federation does not share the belief in human autonomy put forward by the utilitarian school (either the liberal or socialist wing of this 'ethical' philosophy).

In our opinion it is not the concept of self-determination and human autonomy but the idea of religious dependence that is decisive. In this connection we emphasize the norm of stewardship. Stewardship means that not man but God is the owner of creation. It implies that man is not a law unto himself but that he should be obedient to and follow the voice of his Master and Creator to achieve justice and peace for himself and his fellow man. The Lord asks man to be at His disposal, in His service, and to refrain from serving idols. Therefore, powers of evil leading to injustice, unrighteousness and self-interest must be opposed.

4. Some consequences for social ethics

The Christian approach to ethics and trade unionism as described above has far-reaching consequences upon the way we structure the relationship between employers and workers in general and their role and position in the enterprise in particular.

1. According to the Bible, every human being is created in God's own image. This means the full recognition of human dignity and the granting of responsibilities to each person according to his abilities and capabilities.
2. The teachings of the Bible are not limited to personal, individual ethics and attitudes. They also require a policy into which social ethics are fully integrated. The Gospel does not contain a promise and a message to the individual only. It also gives real perspectives for the renewal of society. It stimulates an attitude of structural criticism.
3. Social justice, mercy, righteousness, freedom and responsibility – notions of a high spiritual and ethical value – have to be translated into concrete terms and structures.
4. Structural criticism is the task of both employers and workers. They are together responsible for the proper functioning of the enterprise and the well-being of all persons belonging to that enterprise. Trade unions and employers' associations can have a constructive influence on each other, providing they accept each other as legitimate and equal partners.
5. The Federation rejects the spirit of capitalism because of its unlimited self-interest and its granting of priority to economic aims and targets. Economic and financial power should be used first of all for the promotion of human interests.
6. The Federation cannot accept the modern (neo-Marxist) philosophy of class struggle which provides no real solution for the multiplicity of problems we are faced with today. Emphasizing the antithesis between capital and labour leads to a struggle for power which will result mainly in a shift of power of a very tenuous equilibrium.
7. The attitudes or approaches mentioned in 5 and 6 will undoubtedly lead to an

intensification of the mistrust deeply rooted in history. This mistrust hampers the development of a society in which employers and workers can genuinely cooperate and in which they can really experience their mutual responsibility.

8. The renewal of society depends largely on our attitudes. But it depends just as much on the way we build new structures that will grant people full opportunity to exercise their responsibility. Because of monopolistic and authoritarian structures and policies in modern enterprises, workers have been denied the opportunity to act and function as responsible beings. It is not surprising, therefore, that so many of them are completely uninterested in the well-being of the firm. A lack of responsibility will almost automatically result in a lack of interest and concern.

5. The structure of the modern enterprise

Christian-social thinking disagrees with an approach based on the so-called balance-of-power philosophy. This philosophy clashes with the belief that workers as true partners should share responsibility for the aims and purposes of the enterprise. The Federation therefore advocates an industrial structure in which all groups belonging to the enterprise accept their joint responsibility. Relationships within the enterprise should not be based on property, the provision of money or on power as such. Instead they should be based on:
- real partnership;
- close cooperation;
- co-determination;
- co-responsibility.

In practice we see that the industrial organization of many enterprises is geared primarily to efficiency. Any human relations philosophy in which social issues are subordinated to technological developments and economic or financial objectives obstructs the establishment of sound industrial relations. It impedes genuine social interaction, i.e. an open decision-making process in which the workers too, can act as responsible beings.

For these reasons the Federation advocates a structure of enterprise in which the notion of joint management is accepted as legitimate. Joint management must not be identified with self-management as introduced in Yugoslavia and as defended by neo-Marxist thinkers. Joint management, as we see it, is closely related to the social-ethical approach formulated in the preceding paragraphs.

It implies an enterprise in which:
- the interests of all members and groups should be the same, if possible integrated;

- aims and policy are decided together and important decisions are made jointly on the basis of mutual responsibility;
- the profits are equitably shared;
- working conditions and production methods are adapted to people, rather than vice versa;
- economic profit will be only a means of maintaining a working community aiming to serve society as a whole;
- decisions are made and activities evolved which allow for the impact and consequences they have for society.

In this way we seek to contribute to the achievement of a free and responsible society in which controversy, conflict and self-interest are superseded by trust, open-mindedness and a willingness to serve mankind as a whole.

Finally, it means that management, in close cooperation with the workers and trade unions, should pay full attention, more than ever, to the enterprise's policy towards society.

6. A social bill of rights

The concept of mutual responsibility is radically different from the generally prevailing philosophy of countervailing powers. We advocate a positivation of power relations in which employers (irrespective of their various positions and duties) actively promote a social policy where not power and authority but freedom and responsibility are the guiding norms. The enterprise should have its Magna Carta in which human dignity and the equal worth of all are the keywords. It would be unacceptable to subordinate social policy to economic, financial and technical targets. One of the principal aspects of the enterprise's overall policy must be its policy towards society. Neither management nor employees should be allowed to disregard this aspect. They should be committed to it at all levels in order to avoid becoming aloof or apathetic with respect to what is going on in the enterprise.

In order to implement policy towards society in the entire decision-making process, a policy document might be introduced, clearly spelling out that human needs and values play a dominant role in determining and (re)formulating the enterprise's aims and purposes. Such a document, which might be called a social-economic bill of rights, should contain the principles and main objectives of the policy towards society. In his book in the emancipation of the workers, the Federation's president, Jan Lanser, listed the following social objectives:

- to safeguard the continuity of the enterprise;

- to establish and maintain labour relations which embody the carefully tested norms and values of our social development;
- to cooperate in ensuring the full personal development of fellow workers with respect to their working lives;
- to contribute to the material welfare of fellow workers;
- to promote the education of fellow workers via the trade unions;
- to contribute to national prosperity;
- to ensure that economic growth and technological progress do not take place at the expense of mankind (*Mondige mensen, samen verantwoordelijk*, p. 31).

Adoption of such a bill of rights would prevent the policy towards society from becoming dependent on the willingness and personal views of managers who are primarily responsible for personnel policy. They would be committed to it just as they are committed to any other form of decision-making. In other words: the various aspects (such as social, economic, technical and financial aspects) should be considered as horizontally interdependent and integrated. The basic philosophy of the social-economic bill of rights should be elaborated in collective agreements and be differentiated to meet special needs and possibilities at the various levels of enterprise.

In this way the Federation seeks to give expression to such essential qualities of human life as freedom and responsibility. It tries to bring about teamwork and team-spirit, on the basis that each worker's intellectual and practical potentialities should be used as responsibly as possible. Every worker should be given the opportunity to use his talents to the full.

Individual ethics are very important. But they must be complemented by social ethics. Nobody, whether manager or worker, can say that he is not responsible for the way we produce goods or provide services or for the way we treat one another. Ethics do not stop at the factory gate. Our day and age is crying out for a reappraisal and reappreciation of our norms and values. It is of crucial importance for us to undertake concerted action so that employers and employees can respond together to the new and urgent demand for industrial ethics. If we fail now, we are bound to be faced with new forms of conflict detrimental to society as a whole.

VI. MORAL POLICY AND PUBLIC POLICY

Maurice A. M. de Wachter

1. The ethical component in public policy?

Recent discussions (ca. 1972–1976) on biomedical research into the human fetus, especially in the United States, illustrate the process of decision-making. Every decision presupposes a scale of values which establish priorities.[1] For some, this proves that all decisions are rooted in ethics. However, the difference between the eventual outcome of strictly moral policy decisions on the one hand, and public policy decisions on the other raises the important ethical issue of possibly divergent scales of values being applied in setting priorities. The ethicist, then, would like to know to what extent the ethical component still plays a part in determining public-policy priorities.

One does, indeed, get the impression that a number of factors other than ethical ones play a more important part: for instance the authoritative power of a given medical specialist to make a credible claim of 'critical emergency.' I know of several specialists in obstetrics or gynaecology who complain about financial and other priorities or facilities being given to cardiology and intensive care units, whereas perinatal medicine is threatened by an attitude of indifference by hospital boards. This confirms Freidson's observation that 'within medicine, obviously physical medicine is less likely to be permitted such a regular claim (to critical emergency) than cardiology.'[2] It also confirms my point about competing factors besides the ethical component. Furthermore, the impression that the ethical component only plays a somewhat secondary role in public-policy priorities could be reinforced by many other examples. For example, stances favouring the use and legalisation of marijuana are largely a manifestation of prior, basically underlying ideological commitments. Scientific truth or falsity seem to have little or no impact on the positions that people adopt. Even the

---

1. LeRoy Walters, Fetal Research and the Ethical Issues, in *The Hastings Center Report* 5 (1975), No. 3, p. 16.
2. E. Freidson, *Profession of Medicine*, New York, 1971, p. 120.

divergence in the various interpretations of the evidence seems to go back upon profound normative differences.[3] It would therefore seem that ethics not only has a limited role, but is being forced into a distorted role. It is being manipulated to fit into certain sets of priorities predetermined elsewhere.[4] One is far away from internal ethical quality whereby right and wrong are measured and estimated by the good as such and where moral arguments are both rationally and operationally demonstrable, proved workable and therefore acknowledged as guidelines for concrete action.

Our former question, then, about the extent of ethical components in the setting of policy priorities has developed into the more specific concern of finding out *how* it could work *well*, in order to ascertain *that* it can work at all. The answer to how the ethical component of public policy making would operate correctly is certainly not to be found in allowing ethics to preside over the debate. Rather, ethics should contribute in its legitimate place, not higher nor lower, to the making of public policy. True as it may be that ethics do preside over the realm of moral policy, the same does not apply to public policy. If this statement is correct and acknowledged as such, it may become possible to avoid many a sterile debate about issues which belong to moral policy, yet are time and again tackled on the grounds of public policy. I say 'may,' and not all debates will therefore be avoided by making this tenuous distinction between moral and public policy.

In passing, it must be noted that debates at the strict moral policy level sometimes lead to a deadlock from which there is no salvation except with public-policy decisions. Strange though this may seem, it implies a warning against all forms of self-sufficiency even in the ethician.

2. What makes public policy different?

In the past decade or so the responsibility for hemodialysis has been broadened by the inclusion on committees of both lay and medical members. It would seem reasonable to face the societal aspects (implied in the selection of candidates) by calling on those who are less incompetent in the matter than the physician, even though they in their turn are laymen in medical issues. Thus, a combined team

3. E. Goode, Marijuana and the Politics of Reality, in *Journal of Health and Social Behavior* 10 (1969), 83–94.
4. E. Goode, ibid., p. 88 explains how concepts of 'true' and 'false' are being distorted by social and cultural lenses. He then goes on to say that this does not mean that 'no research has ever been conducted which approaches scientific objectivity.... It is to say, however, that *not all participants in the marijuana controversy have been trained as scientists, nor do they reason as scientists*' (my italics). This used to be a strong argument against *lay* participation in *policy-setting* and determination of priorities, e.g. in the jury model.

would be able to apply a double criterion: (1) the medical-psychological; and (2) the social-moral rehabilitation aspect. Beecher gives the example of 'a 32-year old man with a stable history of employment and responsibility and a family of six to support [who] was chosen over a 45-year old widow whose children were grown up and had left home.'[5] In the process of choosing candidates a set of norms or principles is followed.

In one programme the principle is that the first obligation is to patients already under treatment. Therefore, seen from the viewpoint of management and staff, (1) the decision about the next candidate occurs only when a place becomes available; (2) a new patient is not accepted until the last one has been well launched, for experience has shown that most difficulties occur in the early weeks of treatment; and (3) a new patient is not accepted when any staff shortage exists. From the patient's view his social status, family size, age etc. will be considered. However, as Beecher himself points out, 'a definition of suitability for dialysis depends on a number of factors, some arbitrary, some empiric.'[6] In other words, whoever chooses also sets a priority. From the ethical viewpoint some attention should be directed toward principles and rules guiding these choices of public policy. Are they strictly ethical, or medical, or political, or popular? Or perhaps a combination of all of these?[7]

I would like to advance the following hypothesis: any decision which is guided by only one of these criteria is most likely to be unfair. In my opinion the hypothesis would also apply to any monopoly claim of ethics with regard to these decisions. As is often the case, the best is the enemy of the good. Certainly in a pluralistic society, policy makers 'seek to accommodate a variety of belief systems and interests rather than elevating the views of one single group to the status of national policy. Policy-making also attempts to achieve maximal continuity with some of the generally accepted principles within the society. Finally ... (they) seek to ensure that national policies are formulated and expressed in terms that are clearly understandable to the public at large.'[8] This quotation allows us to

5. H. K. Beecher, *Research and the Individual: Human Studies*, Boston, 1970, p. 142 ff.
6. H. K. Beecher, ibid., p. 143. The fact that some selection committees operate with the norm of 'church-belonging' as a sign of greater social involvement and, therefore, greater worth to the community has been greatly criticized. See: P. Freund, *Experimentation with Human Subjects*, London, 1972.
7. Nobody fails to see that Beecher's description reveals a clear preeminence of medical criteria. Compare with Goode's opinion that only expert scientists should participate in policy-setting. Compare also with E. Freidson, op. cit., p. 5 who sees this as the main characteristic of medicine today: prestige and expert authority make physicians within official policy-making positions lords and rulers, with no rivals or competition.
8. LeRoy Walters, op. cit., 16. The author also offers a good example of such policy deployment of a moral principle. 'Non-therapeutic fetal research should be done only to the extent that such research is permitted on children or on fetuses which will be carried to term' (p. 15).

remark in passing on the fact that the ethical dimension seems to contain a variety of beliefs. Such pluralism constitutes a problem of its own. While fully acknowledging the importance of this question we will not deal with it at this point. Rather, it is the role given to ethics (be it in one or many varieties of belief) which remains the focal point of our interest. What do policy makers do with moral policy decisions when they have to set their priorities?

By now, we have become familiar with the distinction between moral policy and public policy. The remainder of this second point, then, will try to summarize what we know about it. Moral policy and public policy are both related and distinct.[9] With their interest geared mainly towards the ethical component of public policy decisions, ethicians are often tempted to treat their wishes as real: affirming that moral policy constitutes the ethical component of public-policy decisions. Yet a number of other principles equally guide public-policy makers, as, for example, feasibility within this given society. With regard to this feasibility McCormick rightly points out that 'ultimately public policy must find a basis in the deepest moral perceptions of the majority or, if not, at least in principles the majority is reluctant to modify.'[10] He thus joins LeRoy Walters, who said that public-policy makers attempt to achieve maximal continuity with some of the generally accepted principles within society. McCormick further states that public-policy makers, or rather their policy, will not infrequently go beyond morality. And he suggests this is dangerous because 'while one might morally justify this or that experimental procedure on the fetus, the danger of abuse or miscalculation might be so considerable as to call for a policy-ban, or safe-side regulatory cautions.'[11]

While agreeing with the basic contention that moral policy and public policy are related and distinct, I would tend to underline more strongly that there is an 'ought' for moral policy which is not, nor ought to be, one and the same for public policy.[12]

It seems as though McCormick grounds his distinction primarily on the fact that moral policy is concerned with the right and wrong of our (individual?)

9. At the outset of this discussion I wish to follow rather closely the line of an exposé by R. A. McCormick, Fetal Research, Morality, and Public Policy, in Hastings Center Report 5 (1975), No. 3, 26–31.

10. Ibid., 16.

11. Ibid., 16.

12. McCormick sees this too: 'I emphasize here that I am discussing for the present a moral position (not immediately what public policy ought to be) and one that reflects my own views.' (op. cit., 28). Nevertheless, P. Ramsey holds quite different views as he believes that 'a searching inquiry into the morality of fetal research must be the foundation of fetal politics, if it is to be good politics' (Ethics of Fetal Research, New Haven, 1975, p. 72). The difference between these two positions is not just a matter of more or less, but is rather substantial.

conduct whereas law or public policy is guided by the common good.[13] I am not convinced that it is sufficient to explain the distinctness and relatedness of moral policy and public policy by attributing to them respectively 'right and wrong' and the 'common good.' The difference, in my view, is that moral policy is always about morals and nothing else, whereas public policy is about morals and many other things which definitely cannot be reduced to morals. Therefore, the distinction does not hold on the basis of ethical elements (different though these may be in either policy), but it comes from elsewhere. I would look for a distinction along the lines of interaction of moral policy and public policy. Moral policy always being about right and wrong, be it individual or common, should try and offer *relevant* ethics for the public-policy makers. The presence of moral policy in public policy should be proved by its usefulness to the public-policy makers. On the other hand, public policy should care about moral policy in such a way that there is some proportion (of moral quality!) between the (temporary) postponement of some ethical conviction and the common good to be achieved in this way. A further important remark concerns this postponement. It can never mean anything but postponing one good after another good. Thus, it cannot mean that evil is chosen above good, nor that the postponed good is really being destroyed. All of this concerns that which I would like to see present in public policy and may be understood as an endeavour to integrate moral and non-moral elements.

Perhaps this view of the distinction between moral policy and public policy is illustrated in the stances taken by different politicians in different countries with regard to recent debates on the legalization of abortion. Some politicians, though personally against it, sometimes reach a critical point in policy making where they vote for legalized abortion, thereby hoping to reduce the losses to a minimum. Thus, for instance, Norman St.-John Stevas, a British MP and a Roman Catholic, voted (after a long struggle) in favour of the Abortion Bill, and was thus able to help to build a conscience clause into the Act.

3. Fetal research

Recent developments in fetal research and its repercussions on public-policy discussions will be the topic of this third section.

---

13. The approach taken by P. Ramsey would hardly need such a distinction, since moral policy is the root of public policy. Ramsey has no need for two principles. As was said in the previous footnote, Ramsey would consistently deny the question we keep asking about the extent to which moral policy should be present in public policy.

The recent history of this development in the USA is linked with three public-policy documents: (1) The Sir John Peel Report, a British document from 1972 which inspired (2) a series of Provisional Guidelines issued by the NIH (National Institute of Health) under the title *Protection of Human Subjects* (1973). However, Congress intervened and prevented promulgation of these guidelines. It appointed a Commission for the Protection of Human Subjects. A number of judges and lawyers had warned the NIH that they would never support permissive guidelines in matters of fetal research. Subsequently a revised, unexpectedly more permissive edition of the guidelines appeared as (3) the DHEW-NIH guidelines (Department of Health, Education, and Welfare) in 1974.[14]

An interesting example of public policy recommending another course of action is to be found in a statement made by the Executive Director of the American Citizens Concerned for Life, Inc. before the Senate Subcommittee on Constitutional Amendments, August 21, 1974. In part, it reads as follows:

Proper concern for the rights of the unborn child need not bring medical research to a halt. New therapeutic techniques can be used with the hope of proving them superior to traditional methods of treatment, after adequate theoretical work and animal experimentation has been carried out. Parents can give consent for experimental therapeutic treatment of the unborn if there is valid reason to believe that such treatment is in the best interest of the child. In addition, organs may be transplanted from the dead fetus, and tissue cultures may be developed from fetuses which are clinically judged to be dead according to the same criteria which would be used for a born child or adult. We recommend careful retrospective clinical and statistical study of defective babies for identification of teratogenic drugs. However, this is not the same thing as purposefully introducing known or suspected harmful substances for research purposes into the live unborn child or his mother which could cross the placental barrier. Systematic benefit should not be derived from systematic induced abortion. We do not approve of experiments which would be judged 'cruel' or 'senseless' by the average sensitive layman. And parents cannot consent to non-therapeutic research on unborn children who are being purposely aborted.[15]

Obviously this kind of statement illustrates Ramseys contention that morality must be the foundation of fetal politics. To the extent that this recommendation bases public policy in morality it is more relevant for our previous discussion in point two than it is for the present survey. Its value, at this informative stage, lies precisely in its enumeration of several types of fetal research, even though they contain mainly the ones disapproved of by a particular group.

---

14. A more detailed description is given by P. Ramsey in *The Ethics of Fetal Research*, New Haven, 1975, pp. 1–20. Equally important and giving a broader historical context is R. M. Veatch, Human Experimentation Committees, in *Hastings Center Report* 5 (1975), No. 5, 31–40.
15. Quotation from P. Ramsey, op. cit., pp. 72–73.

A somewhat more systematic way of dealing with the policy questions of fetal research can be found in a division used by many authors, viz. into three types of research depending on where the fetus is situated: in the womb, on its way out, or already outside the womb. An instance of the latter type occurs when non-viable fetuses are kept alive artificially in order to develop survival techniques.[16]

This latter example also allows us to link the present section with the often repeated distinction between moral policy and public policy. The public-policy statement is abstractive, i.e. it ignores among other things, such as how the fetus was acquired and where the line of viability is to be drawn. Indeed, public policy regulations do not make any distinction between fetuses procured by miscarriage, provoked abortion, or premature birth. Moral policy, on the other hand, would certainly use this information and subsequently apply the ethical criteria of 'cooperation.'[17] The same can be said about the use of the viability criterion. The Peel Report sets a time boundary at 20 weeks, while the NIH chooses for the 'safe-side of viability.' Both are public-policy statements. Ramsey, on the contrary, and consistent with his basic conviction, makes a primarily moral policy statement in favour of policies in which 'all viable or potentially viable fetuses be treated equally'[18] and he protests against the safe-side criterion because it leaves an intolerable vacuum in the law.

A few very perceptive remarks on the relationship between moral policy and public policy have been made by a lawyer with some experience of state legislature, W. D. Delahunt.[19] He contends that 'the legislature accurately mirrors the composition of the community ... in terms of intelligence, sophistication, philosophy, ethics, and *attitudes regarding* public morality.' About the legislative process itself he has this to say: '... it is certainly deliberative and clearly seeks out input from interested parties as a result, in most cases, of its own lack of expertise. It responds more readily to organized interest groups. *Legislation* which it produces usually reflects a *compromise* of divergent interests within the community.'[20] I think this is a wonderful statement in that it candidly admits that legislators, because of their lack of expertise, expose themselves to the struggle for power by interested groups and therefore produce a compromise. It is admirable in its honesty. Whereas most 'scientists' tend to fill in their lack of

16. Such an allowance is in fact made by one of the regulations issued on July 29, 1975 by the Secretary of Health, Education, and Welfare.
17. See, e.g., R. A. McCormick, Fetal Research, Morality, and Public Policy, in *Hastings Center Report* 5 (1975), No. 3, 28: '... since there is such profound division on the moral propriety of abortion, the moral notion of cooperation in an abortion system will not function at the level of policy.'
18. P. Ramsey, op. cit., p. 60.
19. W. D. Delahunt, 'Biomedical Research: A View from the State Legislature,' in *Hastings Center Report* 6 (1976), 25–26.
20. Ibid., p. 25 (italics mine).

expertness by calling upon 'experts,' the legislator (who is ultimately the public-policy maker) calls upon the representation of interests.

4. Doctors, experts, politicians or laymen?

Whereas traditionally the *professional* committee assisted public-policy makers, the record of the last decade shows a constantly increasing number of lay participants. All committees, so it seems, ought also to become *representative*. Thus the interdisciplinary professional group (each member with special skills to contribute to the commission's deliberations) which already recognized the need for more than one skill is now being superseded by the jury model. While the interdisciplinary model still works along the lines of different kinds of expertise, requests are now being made to admit unskilled members whose only ability is 'to reflect the common sense of the reasonable person'[21] (this is the *jury*), or to perceive and communicate the views of the constituents (this is the *representative* model).

Currently, the human experimentation committees 'are beginning to look very much like interdisciplinary groups of professionals, but there are clear signs of movement toward the jury or at least the representative model.'[22] Delahunt even links this trend with the Age of Consumerism:

The community is now demanding scrutiny of areas that heretofore were immune from review or criticism. Through its legislative bodies the public is insisting that it participate in – even dominate – policies directly affecting business, the professions and governmental agencies. ... I believe that consumerism will not recede but become more militant.[23]

The characteristics of the interdisciplinary team are to be found in the National Committee for the Protection of Human Subjects of Biomedical and Behavioral Research (July 12, 1974). As we already know, Congress meant this committee to be an advisory board or panel, counteracting the provisional guidelines issued by NIH (1973). Innovative is the requirement that a majority be non-researchers.[24] Subsequently other drafts of committees went so far as to reduce the permitted number of researchers to one-third; this somewhat unbalanced reaction was

21. R. M. Veatch, 'Human Experimentation Committees: Professional or Representative?' in *Hastings Center Report* 5 (1975), No. 5, 31–40.
22. Ibid., p. 31.
23. W. D. Delahunt, op. cit., p. 25.
24. The eleven members of the committee are 'distinguished in the fields of medicine, law, ethics, theology, the biological, physical, behavioral and social sciences, philosophy, the humanities, health administration, government, and public affairs.' See R. M. Veatch, op. cit., p. 34.

edged off in the final draft of such groups. Nevertheless, the future will have to show which way society wants to go with decisive authority in policy making.

To sum up, it is useful to locate the types of committees mentioned thus far along a line going from the traditional committee (viz. the professional one) to the general public present in the jury model. Thus we emerge with the following picture (see Figure 1), which incidentally also illustrates the decrease (at least numerically) in expert presence and the increase (again numerically) in general participation of those who might call themselves 'interested' parties.

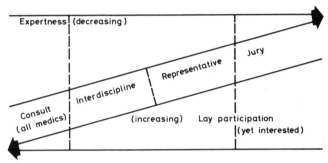

Figure 1

The diagram also reveals a schematic trend in the central area, where about equal parts are allotted to the different parties engaged in a particular situation. It is not my intention to suggest that equal should be understood in the merely quantitative sense of percentages. Rather, the part one should play is measured by the contribution one can make both to diagnoses and treatments, in order for both to be completely adequate for existing needs. Equal then means adequate, not under and not needlessly above the help required. Finally, the primary helpfulness of the diagram may be that it helps to focus discussion on various geographically located structures of decision-making.

In this context it should be remembered that decision- and policy-making owe a lot of their final quality to concrete priorities and to adequate methods and models of precedure. For medical ethics it will be important to weigh the shifts that may occur as one switches the basic models. For instance, what will it mean if the jury model or, what is already happening nowadays, the interdisciplinary model and even to some extent the representative model, operate alongside (or shortly instead of) the professional team of medical experts?

One of the results will be increased 'politicization' of medicine. And, re-markably, another will be 'de-medicalizing' if not of society, at least of policy-making in matters of medicine. The 'losers' in the game will probably be the professionals themselves, i.e. the doctors. If George Bernard Shaw was right in saying that 'every profession is a conspiracy against the laity' then it seems to follow nowadays that lay participation gnaws at professional privileges.

5. The backdrop

Every choice reveals a preference (see Section 1). The inner quality of the choice depends on the adequacy of the method used for reaching the decision (see Section 4). The ethicist is very interested in tracing the *presuppositions* (often unconscious yet undeniably influential) which are the assumptions for a given answer. This final section therefore considers the relationship between one's convictions and one's actions. As such, it is a simple extension of the common saying that people always act according to their beliefs. Though one may readily say with Pascal that whoever does not act according to his beliefs will end up believing according to his actions, I want to highlight only one aspect of this interplay between conviction and action, viz. from belief to action.[25]

Given this limitation, I contend that the causal influence of beliefs upon action gradually weakens as one makes the transition from moral policy to public policy. This weakening seems to occur in different stages:

1. The loss of (contended) causal influence from conviction upon action is least in moral policy which does not have to act by extending itself into public-policy action.

2. The loss becomes somewhat greater as one experiences a conflict between conviction and action.

3. The real loss occurs as soon as the action is no longer determined by the moral policy of either one person or one homogeneous group but by public policy involving many individuals, many groups. 'Tot capita tot mores' may have its most updated translation in our 'pluralistic society.' It is this third type of weakened linkage which is the topic of our moral concern and discussion in this paper.

It would seem possible to present fairly systematically the influence convictions and beliefs have upon the formation of certain decisions and stances with

25. H. Jonas presents similar insights regarding one of the principles at stake in experimentation: '*On principle*, it is felt, human beings ought not to be dealt with in that way (the 'guinea pig' protest) ... Putting the matter thus we have *already made* an important *assumption rooted in our* 'Western' cultural *tradition*. The prohibitive rule is, to that way of thinking, the primary and axiomatic one; the permissive counter-rule, as qualifying the first, is secondary and stands in need of justification. We must justify the infringement of a primary inviolability, which needs no justification itself; and the justification of its infringement must be by values and needs of a dignity commensurate with these to be sacrificed' (in P. A. Freund, op. cit., 3; italics mine).

regard to abortion, for instance. The following scheme may furnish the backdrop against which we will understand the movement described as a gradual weakening of the influence moral policy has in the context of public policy. In its simplest form the diagram should show the answers given when the previous answers are put under pressure, when they are not taken for granted. For instance:

Question:	Abortion?
Answer:	No!
Question:	Why not?
Rule of thumb:	The fetus has a right to live (or: abortion is murder).
Question:	Why not give up the fetus which conflicts with the mother?
Principle:	All life is sacred.
Question:	Why?
View of man (philosophy):	Man belongs to a (divine) law of nature.

This diagram is, of course, an abstraction. Real debates never proceed along these lines. They jump back and forth, mix the arguments and, first and foremost, jump to their own conclusions. The value of this diagram lies in its capacity to show the link between conviction and action. Also, by turning it sideways we get a more abstract and hence more generally applicable presentation of what goes on whenever people argue and defend their stances by referring to their convictions.

Question/Answer ← Rule of thumb ← Principle ← View of man/society

---

We thus develop a diagram which can be filled in according to the topics discussed.[26] We shall also have to allow for the fact that for some people the links

26. As an illustration of the applicability of the diagram, we can consider the following, by P. A. Freund in his *Experimentation with Human Subjects*. He discusses the Seattle case about selection of candidates for hemodialysis. The *principle* upon which the decision had to be made was 'worth to the community' (e.g. church attendance). Freund then made the following objection: 'My own submission was that in a matter of choosing for life and death, not involving specific wrongdoing, no one should assume the responsibility of judging comparative worthiness to live on the basis of unfocused criteria of virtue and social usefulness, and that either priority in time, or a lottery, or a mechanical selection on the basis of age should be followed.'
Note that in this statement the *principle* of worth is discarded and a *rule of thumb* for concrete action is presented (a lottery, etc.). This rule itself is justified by what I would call another *principle*, viz. 'The more nearly total is the estimate to be made of an individual, and the more nearly the consequence determines life and death, the more unfit the judgement becomes for human reckoning' (Ibid, p. XVII).

have to be logical (inductive or deductive) whereas others prefer intuitive links; still others trust their feelings, if not their 'vibes,' and so forth. Thus, while it gives us some clarification at a somewhat abstract level, it should be relativized as far as its true expression of reality is concerned. Nevertheless, as a tool, it will help and even sustain critical reflection in both abstract and concrete situations. Hence its worth.

One may rightly observe that the diagram applies mainly to the formation of moral-policy decisions. What about public policy, especially the way public policy interferes with this? As stated previously, the initial influence public policy has upon this moral policy diagram is one of erosion, a weakening of the connections at all levels. One major exception to the rule might be the monolithic society, where all members are of one mind and one heart. In this, public policy would hardly have any reason not to follow the line proceeding from a common belief (for instance in God as experienced in a given community at a particular point in history) on to the concrete answer 'Thou shalt not kill' (meaning not your own people). But except for ghettos and totalitarian ideologies such situations hardly belong to our daily experience. Public policy has always been biased by its publicity, it has always lacked the privacy of intimacy of conscience. It was always meant to move in the open, and for all. No wonder it lost some of the fine privileges moral-policy makers enjoy. But should it be blamed for that? Should its 'compromise' of necessity be judged immoral or would public policy perhaps deserve to share moral policy's privilege to commit the 'moral compromise'?

VII. POWER AND LEGITIMATION

Willem L. van Reijen

1. Introduction

If you turn the idealistic notion of thinking around, you may get the materialist notion of working, but never the idea of violence, said Hannah Arendt. She analyses the origin of power and violence and their celebration and damnation in social theory.

Our political history is a history of power and violence. 'Politics is the struggle for power, potentiated power is violence' says C. Wright Mills, who placed himself in the line of Machiavelli, Bacon, Max Weber and Trotsky, just to mention some political theoreticians. As a matter of fact, a brief look at our history shows that there has not been one month without war.

Learning history still means learning about wars and emperors more than about the development of our culture. This, considered together with the way politics is presented nowadays in the newspapers as lying and brutal power effects presented (together with the ideology of a free democratic system which we ought to be proud of), makes it almost impossible for our citizens and youth to interpret our society in any terms other than those of power and violence.

Regarding our youth we may think that there are still 'reservations' organised along different lines. Closer observation makes it clear that we are faced with conditions that have to be fulfilled in order to guarantee the powerful organisation of our social process. Besides, these 'reservations' are also full of power and constraints; it might only be more difficult to recognise and analyse them, as they are an integral part of our social experience, so that they do not even appear in our consciousness. But anyhow – our happy youth, free from constraints and material sorrows (non-existent for most of the world population), is then mainly defined negatively, by the absence of the terror of the subsequent working conditions. No one would ever think of applying the conditions of his youth to later organisation forms of social interaction.

This separation of youth and profession, of culture and history is so self-evident to us that we usually do not think about it, and it is even difficult to be aware of it.

Machiavelli recommended his 'principle' of 'Lies for the soul, violence for the body' to domesticate his people. Our society seems to be the perfect embodiment of this principle. A protest against it is liable to appear false, representing a communistic ideology, or a moral appeal. Recent history shows that the two are close together, or even identical in the eyes of a reactionary press.

Indignation and casting blame on their own ideology of freedom and democracy often comes from those who are the victims of this ideology. In our system no one can afford to be a victim, to have lost, because everything is expressed in terms of gain and loss. This means that even the permanent losers are forced to interpret their losses as gains to themselves as well as to others. Those who have nothing to lose but their hope of improving their position are the most fervent defenders of a system that only gives them this hope.

Somebody pointing out an injustice is in danger of being pointed at as the one who caused the trouble. And those who cause trouble risk being considered 'maladjusted.' Someone who cannot adjust himself to the rules of the game (in a system equally 'open' to all of us) is 'out.'

The fact that social processes are organised on the lines of power cannot be only a subject for moral indignation, being itself a result of the power relations which require a moral point of view to legitimate one's own practice. This may be one of the reasons why moral points of view clashing to harshly with day-to-day practice are and must be tolerated. On the other hand, it is clear that moral reasoning alone has never basically changed political conditions under which it was tolerated. That is why Amnesty International considered objectively (and I am not disputing its positive results) has the disadvantage of giving the impression that moral arguments might change a political system. In the case of Amnesty International, politics and morals are posed as contrasts. And it seems as if A.I. can win if public opinion supports its goals. This obscures reality, because it is not realised that the prevailing system of morals is an integral part of the power system. A.I. can win 'cases' but cannot change the political structure. This could be demonstrated by the fact that it is only successful in freeing more or less 'prominent' people.

It is most astonishing that, notwithstanding the fact that power and violence are such basic elements in our societal organisation, science has not bothered much about them. The only thing that has been developed along these lines since Marx, Lenin and Stalin is what is known as 'Peace research,' and this is an affectation of the United Nations rather than a token of serious scientific research.

It is hard to say at the moment to what extent this is changing. But it certainly is significant that more interest is being shown in research into the stability of internal political relationships. We used to understand history as developing along certain lines interrupted by crises. Nowadays it seems that development is only possible as a permanent crisis. And in fact many of our political systems are threatened by what is called 'structural crisis.'

The increasing complexity of international relationships, concentrations of power, the increasing economic difficulties are causing administrative problems that cannot be mastered by using power and sanctions. Problem-solving and crisis management need even more than ever a specific means of stabilising the balance of power in a world (or nation) with open, unequally shared power and other unequally divided privileges; they need legitimation of the system. This means that the 'power elite' has to make it clear that the unequal share is nevertheless an advantage even to those who do not get their share. Posed in this way, this is a contradiction which could not be effective if openly stated and demonstrated. This is why legitimation can only be effective when the use of power is covert and legitimation is kept diffuse.

2. Personal and structural violence

Generally speaking, we can say that power (violence) is used when somebody is forced to do something he would not have done if it had not been forced upon him.

Power (we use the term power in a generalised sense, not one limited to physical power) is a notion which expresses a relationship. We can say that somebody uses power in relation to somebody else; i.e., we can state the fact and the direction of the act. It may be secondary if the power is used within formally defined relationships (organisations) or in informal systems (the family). A certain difficulty lies in the fact that it is hardly possible, if indeed it is possible at all, to distinguish overt power from covert power. It is difficult to make this distinction, for instance, in the case of any mental coercion, be it in terms of threats, withdrawing affection or in the form of internalised norms resulting from these two.

Anyhow, the results, of all these actions are basically the same: someone is forced to do something he otherwise would not have done, thus preventing him from acting in accordance with his own interests or even preventing him from seeing what his own interests are. Galtung, defining the use of power, points this out, saying that in such cases the possible self-realisation is more extensive than the real self-realisation.

To elucidate this limitation of possibilities it might be useful to look more precisely at the difference between overt and covert uses of power.

In the case of the overt use of power (and specifically in the case of the use of violence) we see two active subjects. The power may be mental or physical or a combination of both. Purely physical power is hardly conceivable. Only in its most innocent form (e.g. pushing slightly in a crowd), would we be ready to agree that it does not change the mental conditions of the subjects involved to any serious extent. However, even being touched by a policeman, if he lays his hand on my shoulder, may change my emotions. In any case it is certain that physical impacts in more serious forms influence the subject's mental condition. In its most extreme form, this influence will change from hate into identification with the aggressor, as Freud pointed out and as was demonstrated in a macabre way in the Nazi concentration camps. We also know that sensory deprivation as used in the case of the Baader-Meinhof Group in Western Germany and as tested under laboratory conditions has the effect of brainwashing the subject and may lead to the mental distortion known as a change of personality.

The experience of being tortured can result in lifelong suffering, both mentally and physically. Freud and Spitz made an impressive analysis showing that children reveal self-destructive tendencies (they direct hate against themselves) if they do not have the feeling of being loved by somebody. In such cases they may express their basic feelings by nail-biting, stomach aches, and not least by extreme mistrust of others, feelings of insecurity and so on.

These difficulties of distinguishing clearly between external and internal forms of power are no less valid in the case of structural power. First of all, we speak of structural power if we cannot point directly to the agent, even when it is clear that the subjects have been harmed. It will be clear that we speak of harm, not only in its physical aspects, but always when human existence is interfered with. This brings to mind Freud's definition of health, meaning being able to work and to love. We quote this definition, because it attaches equal weight to personal development and social responsibility. It is easy to see that harm, so defined, ranges from illiteracy, asymmetrical sharing of goods (including hunger and in general the problems of the Third World) to asymmetrical sharing of the possibilities of influencing decisions in highly developed industrial nations. Again, combinations are usual. The main index of such structural power is that the people involved can hardly do anything to change their conditions without outside help. This point may help us to see that the practice of power not only means direct action but also implies control of the conditions for the use of power. Again, we would like to draw attention to the fact that people in the Third World who are nearly starving remain victims of the abuse of power even when they get some food. As long as they are dependent they cannot develop according to their own needs and decisions (this is apart from our knowledge that survival alone does not guarantee human life). Children lacking basic elements in their food will have underdeveloped brains, which in turn reduces their capacity for education and professional activities.

The question of whether there is any need for people to starve in this day and age touches the roots of our interpretation of the word 'human,' which means we are not talking simply about partial improvement but about the structural conditions of the use of power, in the awareness that we are asking this question under the conditions we are criticising.

The question of power is itself a phenomenon of using power, albeit indirectly, so that it confronts actual, effected power with the power inherent in the possibility for asking for a legitimation of power. This power to ask for the conditions of the use of power touches on those undiscussed conditions and value systems of our society which might be distorted by discussing them (as is shown by hysterical reactions to trends for liberation in countries under Soviet imperialist influence).

These examples might suggest that the use of power is a normal question where it appears to be a question of consciousness. And indeed, though the question of legitimation points in that direction, we shall nevertheless see that the question of legitimation of the use of power is a question transcending the borderline of theory, as it is, first of all, a practical question. Here I want to emphasize that 'practical' includes consciousness, and that the expression 'practical question' must be regarded as an index; and therefore that we need a theory on the theory-practice relationship focussing on the formation of public opinion as related to social power systems. This leads us to the next question:

3. Can power be legitimated?

Before posing this question it should be asked whether power as such is necessary at all. Political philosophy in recent centuries says it is, and suggests only directives to avoid its misuse. Though the question is too important to accept simple, traditional answers, this is not the place to start a fundamental discussion about this. We are at present discussing only the aspects existing in our society and are not thinking of other possibilities for changing systems of production and so on.

On the other hand, we must agree that asking the question in this way means asking it under conditions of the misuse of power, i.e. by subjects affected in some way by the actual misuse of power (even so, and not in the least, corrupted by the advantages they may have as compared with people in the Third World, for example).

We cannot find an Archimedian point to change the world, and it is true that any criticism is limited by the conditions criticised. But the problem of 'true' criticism should not be transformed into an academic question on the problem of human knowledge. Nor can it be deduced from or reduced to a moral question. The only presupposition we need is the acceptance of a system of reasoning capable of arriving at a consensus between the partners. Though even this can be held to be problematic, an even greater problem is the relation between this 'theory' and practice (see the discussion between the 'Frankfurter Schule' and the Marxists).

Notwithstanding this problem, I should like to try to demonstrate how such a minimal system of reasoning can be found by using Marx's analysis of the exchange of values under capitalistic conditions.

One of the usual misunderstandings about Marx is that he based his analysis on moral judgement, saying that the exchange of wages and 'Arbeitskraft' is unjust and should be changed because of the immorality of unequal exchange. Marx pointed out that this perspective does not hold, because the exchange is at the same time just and unjust. It is just insofar as the capitalist pays for what the worker has given, i.e., his ability to do a certain quantity of work. The 'hands' can renew this ability with the energy (in the form of food, coal, etc.) which they can buy in exchange for the energy they lost by working. When the capitalist argues this way he speaks the truth and does the worker justice. But he does not tell the whole truth and does not do the worker justice because he treats the work he gets as having only an exchange value; in reality the work he gets for his money also has a use-value, i.e., value that has a worth beyond simple exchange value.

The difference between exchange value and use-value (surplus value) was kept by the capitalist. Marx based his analysis on the perception of a society characterised by the existence of wealth, values in the form of goods. And he, as did Smith and Ricardo, wondered where these values came from. In line with his predecessors, he concluded that wealth resulted from work and from work alone. Work alone adds value to the stuff nature offers. But the term 'value' has a double meaning (as indicated) and we have to analyse this double meaning in order to understand what happens when people produce and exchange goods. The term 'goods' has the same double meaning. We can consume the 'goods' (they have consumption value) or we can exchange them (exchange value). Doing one excludes the other, and vice versa. This means that the 'goods,' though 'one,' have two, even contradictory, meanings. This contradiction is not overt; we have to reason to show it. And this reasoning has nothing to do with moral arguments; it is based on the perception of wealth and its explanation.

It is important to see that the explanation of wealth (i.e., of its origin and its increase) is not merely a description systematically listing observed phenomena, but it must also be able to distinguish the appearance of it from the real mechanism. (We take it for granted that the surface of water reflects light in such a way that a stick held in the water seems to be broken. But we know that in the range of social action differences such as those between 'false appearance' and reality also exist.)

Science can be defined as a systematic endeavour to detect such differences in order to control and to foresee future actions. Now, even without a closer examination of Marx's analysis, we can see that our society has an asymmetrical division of wealth and that the disparities are growing, both in our society and in relations between it and the countries of the Third World. The existence of these disparities and their perpetuation has to be legitimated in practice. Otherwise the underprivileged would use violence to change the situation and would take advantage of it (that is to say, they would initiate a revolution).

Concretely, legitimation is the activity that makes people believe that the actual situation with all its disparities is favourable for all the people, even for those who cannot improve their conditions (perhaps it could be called ideology). I suggest that we call such social practices situations in which structural violence occurs. The asymmetrical division of wealth is practised in such a way that there are norms for this unequal division in combination with a system of norms regulating the people's activities, including their silent agreement to this unequal division of socially produced wealth. This might make it clear that it is purposeless to start explaining wealth from the system of norms which is itself one element in the social processes which 'use' norm-systems but are not based on them.

The effectiveness of the norm-system is related to the threat of overt violence (the police, the army) which is clearly related to the internal stability of the various political systems. On the other hand, it is clear that no complex society can exist when there are only permanent overt threats. It is most frequently a combination of the stick and the carrot which is politically effective. This combination is in turn controlled by those who already have structural advances allowing them to influence the forms and often even the times of protests which the government can tolerate. One of the elements upholding this political practice is that existing power relationships cannot readily be made evident, even though they are part of our daily lives. The gap between experience and the possibility of explaining experience is not only a shortcoming in our everyday lives but also in the social sciences. The mere recording of observable facts gives no information on the social (for instance man-made) causes of which the observable facts are manifestations. An out-and-out critic might change our feeling of helplessness, but criticism alone will not change the division of wealth and perhaps cannot even change the conditions for practising science as a critical approach to the hidden mechanisms appearing in the form of norm-systems.

This is the point at which we should clarify what is meant by the statement that science cannot be value-free, which does not mean that non-value-free science would capitulate in trying to find the truth. This topic requires further discussion.

4. Is the problem of legitimation correlated with seeking the truth?

Beyond all kinds of legitimation we can hold a pretention of telling the truth. It is most implausible that people can lie all the time to all other people, knowing and feeling that they are lying. Of course this is not only and not even mainly a psychological problem. What is meant is that, together with the idea of legitimation, there is the implication that speaking is possible only when we assume that other people tell the truth. Without this condition all speaking would be absurd. (We keep this condition even in the knowledge that some people – or even all people – lie sometimes.)

Truth, at least as an ideal, is a basic condition for human interaction. We might even say that all human activity is directed by truth, or what is held to be the truth (again in the knowledge that the contrary may sometimes be the case). This must be so, because otherwise no action whatsoever could take place, action being defined as the possibility of acting in concert with other people, which necessitates a common definition of the situation they are in. It is the very interpretation of the situation (telling the truth about it) which allows the action to be justified, just as the action demonstrates the truth of the interpretation insofar as it is possible to conclude whether the action was successful or not.

We believe it is consistent to compare this 'model' of action and interpretation with the way social systems act and interpret the situations for their 'members.'

Max Weber has pointed out that no administration can survive by using only power and violence, but that it also needs legitimation. Here at least it may be clear that legitimation can be considered as continuing to use power with different means (to adapt Clausewitz's *bon mot* on war).

What can be regarded as the truth depends on the criteria for defining rationality. We describe as rational that which can be accepted by discourse, for example, using reasons which can be accepted by those who are able to understand what is said and to express their reasons in a comprehensible way, direction versus consensus (Habermas). This can be regarded as counterfactual as in the case of people 'always telling the truth.' But this 'ideal' must be accepted because it must exist in order to arrive at a common opinion about the criteria we have just mentioned.

This is undoubtedly circular, but it must be realised that logic can never solve this problem, as logic relates to the possible, significant relations of words but not to reality, which proves that logic employs a limited meaning of truth.

Returning to our main subject, we may say that our society as the asymmetrical, structurally unequal distributor of wealth needs a self-stabilising system of norms which must be legitimated, while the legitimation itself cannot be legitimated. There are no norms to norm the norm (indefinite series). Legitimation is experienced in the form of norms not established rationally but ideologically. This, moreover, is responsible for the fact that they cannot be described in the usual formal scientific way, as 'observable' realities.

The solution practised is to limit the meaning of legitimation to a formal procedure. Hence, in judicial proceedings a definition of justice cannot be asked for; there are only 'facts' subsumed under paragraphs in accordance with rules. Positive right is characterised by the fact that the paragraphs and the rules (as well as the definition of facts) can be changed without provoking a public discussion about the purport of the laws. Justice is done when the procedures have been followed correctly. The same development can be noted in decision-making within the government administration. The existence of procedures may give the impression that it is not persons who are using power, but that there are necessities forcing us to do something. Power appears to be a relic of the feudal past which should be (and can be) eliminated.

It seems to be a relic of nature with its foundations in the biological sphere, just like aggression.

The overt paradox here consists in saying that, in the meantime, culture is specifically human and being human means not simply accepting the nature of man (moral norms, for instance) but also accepting the existence of the striving for power and aggression as unalterable.

It will be obvious that within this contradiction no plausible explanation can be given for the legitimation of the use of power and defining culture as a human product with the goal of improving the 'bad' nature of mankind.

In parenthesis I want to underline this thesis by recalling that nowadays some people (such as Solzhenitsyn) still understand political structure in the form of personalisations. We still hear people talk about the 'born leader' or 'the devil Stalin.' I would not deny the existence of sadists in a world so cruel as we know it, but it should also be realised that all of us together produce a political structure which allows maladjusted persons to acquire positions which permit them to send people to hell.

Again, I am not defending or damning rationality or irrationality, but what I do want to make clear is that there will be antagonism in our society as long as irrational elements can present themselves as rational to our consciousness, and vice versa.

It is this very confusion which makes possible to uncontrolled use of power in our society, while legitimation of the use of power is interpreted as a strictly formal case done justice to as long as procedural rules are followed. Our political system raises a kind of very diffuse loyalty, which makes it possible for many decisions to be taken without the need for politicians to legitimate their acts. This is also demonstrated by the empty slogans at election times, which allow the political parties afterwards to fill them in with concrete laws and regulations whose purport is different from what the populace assumed them to mean.

On the one hand, it must be admitted that this allows a certain flexibility essential in the domain of administration, but it is also clear that the elasticity of the slogans is often used to introduce developments not corresponding to the voters' interests.

It must be said that here there is a certain fight for the definition of rationality (truth) and that it is not clear who has a monopoly in defining rationality: one certainly has the opportunity to put whoever offends him in the range of irrationality, thus eliminating him from participation in the common political system. What should be criticised is that the process and the rules for defining 'rationality' are liable to be handled irrationally. This will persist so as long as the division of power in our society is asymmetric, asymmetry itself being something that cannot possibly be legitimated rationally. In this case we can say things that can be dealt with legally but not legitimately.

VIII. THE SOCIAL RESPONSIBILITY OF BUSINESS

Hein Schreuder

> 'The economists of the laissez-faire school purported to abolish the moral problem by showing that the pursuit of self-interest by each individual rebounds to the benefit of all. The task of the generation now in rebellion is to reassert the authority of morality over technology; the business of social scientists is to help them see both how necessary and difficult that task is going to be' (Joan Robinson, *Freedom and necessity*, 1970).

1. Introduction

The selection of 'Ethics' as one of the four basic themes at a seminar on decision-making in business represents a both hopeful and challenging decision on the part of the organizing committee. As a business economist I must admit that the ethical aspect of decision-making is often lacking in our textbooks and courses. Furthermore, when economists do become involved in matters with an ethical content, the results do not always speak in their favour.[1] Add to these considerations my belief that economics and ethics cannot really be separated, and it will be clear that there is a gap to be bridged.

The aim of this paper is to discuss a concept which might form an element in the bridge: the social responsibility of business. It is a concept which has attracted increasing attention among business economists and which is firmly based in ethics. As an indication of the meaning of this concept, the following definition, which is almost identical to Dilley's,[2] is presented:

---

1. A case in point is the ethically questionable use of the Paretian optimum. See Boulding (1969) and Hicks (1975).
2. Dilley (1974) also includes activities which are considered by law as beneficial to the well-being of society. We regard the legal requirements as the minimum.

Social responsibility is the performance (or non-performance) of activities by a private enterprise without the expectation of direct economic gain or loss, for the purpose of improving the social well-being of the community or one of its constituent groups. These activities are generally recognized by society as beneficial to the well-being of society.

However, before discussing this concept of social responsibility, some attention will first be given to the relation between economic theory and ethics in general. The role values (should) play in economic theory is examined in particular. The reason for this point of departure is the lack of agreement between economists whether concepts with such a large ethical content deserve a place in economic theory.[3] In the following chapter we will find that ethical considerations are generally removed from economic arguments as a consequence of the dominance of the critical-rationalistic school of thought. It seems that the concept of social responsibility serves as an outlet for the dissatisfaction caused by the limitations thus imposed on the economic argument.

2. Economic theory and ethics

The science of economics originated from moral philosophy. Confronted with the division between the two today, this may seem surprising at first glance. However, it is quite comprehensible that the early moral philosophers striving to describe (or better: prescribe) the natural or an equitable organization of society would meet with problems which are nowadays regarded as belonging to the subject-matter of economic science. The way in which a society chooses between its scarce resources shapes its features and its development profoundly. Therefore, the Greek philosophers already concerned themselves, for example, with the distribution of wealth and later philosophers-economists struggled hard to determine a 'just' exchange price for goods.

Notwithstanding 'the fact that the Wealth of Nations does not contain a single analytical idea, principle, or method that was entirely new in 1776,'[4] Adam Smith is generally regarded as the founding-father of economic science. In

---

3. The different positions taken in this discussion seem to be influenced by a difference in ideology too. Cf. 'It is my strong impression that if one were to be told whether an economist was fundamentally sympathetic or hostile to basic capitalistic institutions, especially private property and the related rights to income streams,... one could predict with a considerable degree of accuracy both his general approach in economic theory and which side he would be on in the present controversies' Harcourt (1972) on the Cambridge Controversy.
4. Schumpeter (1954).

retrospect, the honour is justified, but on unexpected grounds: unlike his precursors Smith found it impossible to deal with economics and moral philosophy simultaneously, so he published two separate books on these subjects. General agreement exists nowadays that they should be viewed as a whole. The *Theory of moral sentiments* (1759), however, in which Smith set forth the ethical presuppositions of his economic theory of laissez-faire, never received proper attention from later economists.

The Wealth of Nations became the starting-point of an economic theory from which ethical considerations were removed. Although the subject-matter of economics was expanded in later times, the connection with ethics was not often made.[5] Indeed, the separation was regarded as beneficial to the development of economic theory.

The last statement calls for a reflection on the relationship between economic theory and ethics. The central term in this discussion is 'value judgement.' In line with economic terminology we define a value judgement as a personal preference, implying a ranking of alternatives.[6] Preferences, of course, are the starting point of economic theory. However, it is believed that economic science should not concern itself with an evaluation of preferences. The economist is allowed to introduce hypothetical preferences as a starting point of his economic analysis, but he should not take a moral stand on them. When dealing with the real world, he should only take 'revealed preferences' as an input and at the utmost he may point out an inconsistency of preferences or an 'irrationality' of the decision-maker. He has no dealings whatsoever with the moral aspects of preferences in the real world.

The same 'neutral' standpoint applies to the results of economic analysis. Economic advice should only pertain to the realization of hypothetical or revealed preferences. The economist should only work in an advisory capacity, telling which means will serve the stated ends best. About the economic and non-economic (side-) effects of these means, he should remain morally silent too. This code of conduct has been dominant among economists for a long time.[7] It can be traced back to Max Weber, and its most outstanding modern spokesmen are Karl Popper and Hans Albert. We will follow convention in calling it the 'critical-rationalistic' school.[8] In Holland and Western Germany[9] it is the leading school of thought among business economists, although especially in the

5. The most outstanding exception perhaps is 'welfare economics.'
6. Boulding (1969).
7. Myrdal (1953) clearly demonstrated the impossibility of excluding values from economic theory and revealed the implicit values in the classical theory.
8. Or logical-positivism. Of course only the stand on 'Wertfreiheit' is mentioned here.
9. Cf. Heinen and Dietel (1976) and Fischer-Winkelmann (1971).

latter country it has never quite won the day and opposition is mounting again.

The opposition against the critical-rationalists can be labelled the 'normativistic' school. Normativists claim that a completely value-free economic science is an impossibility. Every man, including economists, looks at the world through the coloured glasses of his value system. And, for instance, the subjects he chooses for research and the assumptions he picks about how reality works (or should work) are motivated by certain values too. Thus, while in theory any assumption, say, regarding business goals is permissible, the 'neutral' standpoint of the critical-rationalist in fact leads to acceptance of the goals of the strongest interest groups in society. In the view of the normativist, the critical-rationalistic concept of science serves the establishment.

Now it is strange to note that in his time Weber was thought of as very progressive. Or is it really so strange? It is well known that Weber fought for the separation of science and politics at a time and in a country where this was very necessary. We shall all be grateful that his efforts were not in vain, because of the unacceptability of the then emerging normative opinions, certainly in scientific reasoning. The example clearly demonstrates that, as such, the abandonment of subjective, moralizing reasoning has indeed been of the utmost importance to scientific development. But what, then, about the normativistic arguments?

In my opinion the two schools are talking at different levels. The critical-rationalists are talking about the relation between the scientist and his science, while the normativists are focussing on the relation between the scientist and his environment, the world or – to express it with a crude technical term – his data. Of course, there are cross-relations, but this distinction gives us a tool to separate the working-spheres of both attitudes. I would submit then that the normativistic attitude applies to the stages in the work of the scientist which closely relate to the outside world: these would be the first and the last stages of his work.[10] In the first stages of his work he conceives of reality and transforms his concept into operational terms and assumptions. In the last stages he has obtained scientific results and should then evaluate the impact of these results on the world. It is a denial of the responsibility of man to expect the economist to disregard his own moral opinion about the phenomena he deals with and about the results of his work. In these stages of his work the normativistic attitude is most 'critical' as it encourages the application of different value systems.[11]

The area left uncovered until now – from assumptions to results – is the realm of the critical-rationalistic view. Here no value judgements should be allowed, for they would then interfere with scientific reasoning: '*de gustibus non est*

10. Perhaps it would be helpful for a synthesis of both schools to call these stages 'extra-scientific.'
11. The relevant values should be made explicit to the extent possible.

disputandum.' It is exactly the separation of facts and values which enables us to form a common ground for argument. During the argument falsification should be possible. Therefore, the flow from assumptions to results should ideally be value-free. Having thus stated our position in this controversy we can move on to find the implications of the concept of social responsibility.

3. The social responsibility of business

Conventionally, economic theory has stressed that the main task of business is to secure as much return as possible on the capital entrusted to it. Differences about the true causes of profit or about a just distribution of it have always been plentiful, but about the need for its creation there is broad agreement. We shall call this the *economic responsibility of business.* A presupposition of this classical goal of business is that firms can discharge other responsibilities, for instance to their workers, by paying a price (wages). In this way, taxes can be regarded as the price a firm has to pay for functioning in a specific community.

When, at the end of the nineteenth century or the beginning of the twentieth, business economics came into being as a specialisation of its own, it was, therefore, only natural that profit maximization (per unit of capital invested and in the long run) was understood to be the primary aim of business. Of course, there was thus close correspondence with the state goal of maximization of national product (or income) and it is needless to say that this orientation has indeed been of paramount importance in a society suffering from material want. In the meantime, other business goals have been recognized, such as continuity, growth, increasing the market-share or the 'value of the firm.' But profit is, of course, a derivative of these goals and has remained the ultimate criterion in business decisions.

The outright pursuance of the economic responsibility of business, however, entails consequences which can be regarded as socially harmful. Moreover, it can distract attention from other, socially relevant goals. It is, therefore, clear that economic action should be restricted in some way in order to minimize or offset the social harms as well as to ensure that the social goals, which cannot be pursued profitably, are nevertheless attained. Historically, these functions have been conferred upon government. In this view business and government are countervailing powers with no common ground. Business should not take on duties which are alien to the profit-motive and government should not interfere with private enterprise for other than the two stated reasons.

Gradually, another view has emerged.[12] According to this view, business itself

12. Heald (1957).

has a social responsibility[13] in addition to its economic responsibility; it should evaluate both the economic and the social results of its activities. This view has been widely accepted with regard to the firm's responsibility toward its workers. In describing the role of labour in a business firm, we no longer use the 'model' of the two separate entities, the worker and the firm, communicating through the labour market. It has been replaced by the 'model' in which the workers are participants in the business firm. They not only exact a monetary reward for their labour, but seek fulfillment in their jobs too. Thus there should be some minimal degree of correspondence between the goal system of the firm and the value system of its participants.

The heart of the debate on social responsibility nowadays lies in the relationship between business and its environment: society at large. In particular possible conflicts between business goals and societal goals are receiving attention. According to an article in *the Wall Street Journal* the current trend is that: '... maximum financial gain, the historical number one objective of American business must in these times move into second place whenever it conflicts with the well-being of society.'[14] Examples of issues in the debate are: product safety, environmental pollution, employment of minorities, urban decay and boycotting certain countries.[15] Indeed, it is quite a varied list. Later on we shall try to attain some orderliness in this field. Let us first see what arguments are presented by the proponents of business involvement in these issues.

The arguments in favour of social responsibility of business generally point to the vast resources business has at its command, the dangers of employing these resources for too narrowly defined a purpose and the possibilities of social progress if private enterprise were to broaden its scope. In short, it is believed that business has a certain amount of power to achieve societal goals. In the classical model of perfect competition this is not the case. The classical firm is completely at the mercy of the market and can only adapt to its whims. Therefore, many proponents of social responsibility set out to show that the classical model no longer holds good. The chief reason for its being outdated is the growth business firms have shown and the increasing degree of concentration in many markets. Furthermore, some assumptions of the classical model appear to be no longer correct; for instance, the assumption that market prices are accurate indicators of societal desires.

The power business thus supposedly possesses is felt to be at least partially misdirected for two reasons:

13. See the definition in paragraph 1.
14. Malabree (1971).
15. Jacoby (1974).

1. *incomplete analysis of relevant consequences of business decisions.* Environmental consequences, for instance, are left out of the analysis because the environment lacks a market-price. Economic theory still struggles with 'externalities,' uncompensated consequences of economic action of an entity for third parties or society at large.
2. *too narrow a confinement of business goals.* Adam Smith already recognized that the criterion of wealth maximization cannot be applied to all socially desirable activities.[16] Business has been very successful in performing the tasks it has taken on. It is felt that this very success has led to an overemphasis on profitable activities, which is clashing more and more with other social goals.

The above distinction is very important. As one can imagine, when the reasons for demanding a social responsibility of business differ, the actual content of the demands differs too. Generally, however, the two different demands are lumped together, which makes fruitful discussion virtually impossible. This has been done in our introductory definition too. It reads: 'Social responsibility is *the performance (or non-performance)* of activities by a private enterprise ...' This clearly involves two different forms of social responsibility:

1. *restraining:* business is asked not to perform certain activities, although these promise to be profitable in a traditional economic analysis. However, when social consequences are taken into account, it is felt that the social harms outweigh the economic gains.
2. *activating:* business is asked to perform certain activities with no expected economic gain because of the resulting social benefit. Thus business is required to take on social goals independent of its economic goals.

The activating social responsibility precedes the economic analysis, as it influences the process in which goals are selected. The restraining form is a complement to the economic analysis in which economic and non-economic factors are evaluated and weighed. With this distinction in mind it is instructive to see what arguments are brought forward against social responsibility. Although heavily outnumbered by proponents of the concept, there have always been ardent opponents too. Their line of reasoning mostly has the same starting-point: the power of business. However, it is then argued that, precisely because of its power, business should not assume responsibilities other than its traditional economic ones.

16. Smith (1971).

Hayek, for instance, states:

If the large aggregations of capital which the corporations represent could, at the discretion of management, be used for any purpose approved as morally or socially good, ... this would turn corporations from institutions serving the expressed needs of individual men into institutions determining which ends the efforts of individual men should serve. To allow the management to be guided in the use of funds, entrusted to them for the purpose of putting them to the materially most productive use, by what they regard as their social responsibility, would create centres of uncontrollable power never intended by those who provided the capital.[17]

Of course, Hayek continues, such power would not be left uncontrolled:

So long as the management is supposed to serve the interest of the stockholders, it is reasonable to leave the control of its action to the stockholders. But if the management is supposed to serve wider public interests, it becomes merely a logical consequence of this conception that the appointed representatives of the public interest should control the management.

Levitt follows this line too, but pushes a bit farther ahead still: 'In the end the danger is not that government will run business or that business will run government, but rather that the two of them will coalesce into a single power, unopposed and unopposable.'[18] Business, therefore, should stay 'narrowly profit-oriented,' because otherwise 'in its guiltdriven urge to transcend the narrow limits of derived standards, the modern corporation is reshaping not simply the economic but also the institutional, social, cultural and political topography of society.' In short: the fear for a corporate society.

Both critics have been so extensively quoted to make it clear that their attacks regard only the activating form of social responsibility. Both actually contend that in fulfilling its economic tasks business should stay within the framework of morality. So there seems to be no opposition to the concept of a restraining social responsibility. And quite rightly so: if, as the opening quotation from Joan Robinson suggests, economic theory has seemed to teach that no moral problems were involved in the pursuit of self-interest, as this aim automatically leads to the greatest benefit for all, it is fortunate to see that economists speaking out on the subject have not been misled and do not differ in the prominence given to morality.

What remains, then, is the question whether business should perform activities resulting in a social benefit but at an economic loss. Of course, it is appealing to give an affirmative answer to this question, considering how much has yet to be accomplished in the social field. However, I believe we should not require

17. Hayek (1969).
18. Levitt (1958).

business to pursue social goals which would conflict with its economic goals. Business has the primary task of putting capital to its most productive use, thereby contributing to the welfare of society. If we take a world-wide view, there remains very much to be done in the fields where business traditionally operates too. Furthermore, it is a matter of making clear choices: do we want specific economic benefits or specific social benefits?; do we want private goods or public goods? and so on. When economic and social goals are pursued by one and the same organization, there is a real danger that no clear-cut choices will be possible, but only 'package deals.' It should be clear, too, how the choices are made. The setting of social goals and the decisions on social policy should be the outcome of a social process in which all possibly affected can participate. Especially with regard to decisions with effects transcending the interests of the local community, it is difficult to see how such a process could be institutionalized in business. Finally, it is good to realize that asking business to perform social activities at an economic loss implies approval of its performing economic activities at a greater economic profit than strictly necessary.

So, in conclusion, I propose to use the term 'social responsibility' only in its restraining sense.[19] It is then intended to convey that social and moral considerations are a natural and necessary complement to economic analysis. Business economists should keep on stressing that a purely economic analysis is not the whole story. Economic theory cannot give a complete recipe for economic action in the real world, because the businessman has to make all kinds of valuations and has to include many more considerations in his decision-process than economists can afford in their theoretic models. Therefore, the businessman cannot take value-free decisions based only on economic theory. The step from theory to reality requires the application of values. We have seen in paragraph 2 that this holds for economists as well. The debate on social responsibility of business really is about these values and the process of their application. The participants, therefore, should not only be businessmen and economists.

19. When we mean the activating sense (that business should include social goals in its goal-system) we could speak of 'social activism.'

References

Boulding, K. E., 1969, Economics as a moral science, *American Economic Review*, March.

Dilley, S. C., 1974, What is social responsibility?, *CA Magazine*, November.

Fischer-Winkelmann, 1971, *Methodologie der Betriebswirtschaftslehre*, W. Goldmann Verlag, Munich.

Harcourt, G. C., 1972, *Some Cambridge controversies in the theory of capital*, The University Press, Cambridge.

Hayek, F. A., 1969, The corporation in a democratic society: in whose interest ought it and will it be run? in H. I. Ansoff, *Business strategy*, Penguin.

Heald, M., 1957, Management's responsibility to society: the growth of an idea, *Business History Review*.

Heinen, E. and B. Dietel, 1976, Zur 'Wertfreiheit' in der Betriebswirtschaftslehre, *Zeitschrift für Betriebswirtschaft*, Jan./Feb.

Hicks, J. R., 1975, The scope and status of welfare economics, *Oxford Economic Papers*, November.

Jacoby, N. H., 1974, The corporation as social activist, in S. P. Sethi, *The unstable ground: corporate social policy in a dynamic society*, Mellville, Los Angeles.

Levitt, T., 1958, The dangers of social responsibility, *Harvard Business Review*, Sept./Oct.

Malabree, A. A., 1971, The outlook: appraisal of current trends in business and finance, *The Wall Street Journal*, Vol. CLXXVII, No. 55.

Myrdal, G., 1953, *The political element in the development of economic theory*, Routledge and Kegan Paul, London.

Schumpeter, J. A., 1954, *History of economic analysis*, George Allen and Unwin, London.

Sethi, S. P., 1974, *The unstable ground: corporate social policy in a dynamic society*, Melville, Los Angeles.

Smith, Adam, 1971, *The wealth of nations*, Penguin.

IX. A RECONNAISSANCE INTO TECHNOLOGY AND ETHICS

Antoine Kreykamp

Ethical considerations are often experienced as pious afterthoughts. Or worse, as the doctor after death, or a balancing item on the budget. Yet, as I hope to show, this impression does not reflect the true state of affairs. It is an assumption, based on the obvious fact that completely different tools are required to handle ethical problems than are needed, for instance, for budgetary, technical or organizational matters. In the latter case both the issues and the tools are called 'hard' whereas ethical considerations are called 'soft' which, with the views prevailing today, borders on disqualification.

Now I have been writing in the preceding paragraph as if we were quite clear and unanimous as to what is meant by ethical considerations. Yet a single random sample, or even the early stages of a discussion would provide sufficient proof of the absence of this supposed clarity and unanimity. Confusion of tongues and communication failures are greatly in evidence. No definition or description I might present here would change this situation, let alone improve it. After all, the possibility that we shall understand one another is not to be found in the field of definitions or descriptions, but on the terrain we cross before reaching these: that of experience. For this reason I want to start with a typical example of a situation in which people feel themselves confronted by ethical problems.

1. A challenging offer

Suppose that a firm of technical consultants is offered a commission by one of the oil producing and exporting countries. It involves the design of an entire naval port with all its road connections to the hinterland and so on. Little imagination is required to picture the receipt of this invitation in the present economic situation. The first reaction of the management, anxiously conscious of its responsibility for the continuity of the firm and full employment for all its employees, is one of satisfaction at such an exceptionally favourable opportunity. Yet at the same time several directors express their doubts. This is, after all, a purely military and strategic project, and taking part in it will give rise to complications. This aspect is shown up in their uncertain manner when the management informs its employees about the commission.

Reactions vary greatly. Some people regard the commission as a challenge to their capability as designers and foresee the possibility of future promotion. Others are on the point of revolt at the idea that they would have to participate in a strategic military project. The general mood drops to zero when one of the employees declares with emotion 'As a Jew I am not allowed to enter their country and I refuse to work for them.' This makes others realise that they will probably have to produce an official statement of being non-Jewish if the project takes them to that country.

In such a situation the questions posed are no longer academic. Nor are they the type of questions intended to keep a discussion going. The problems involved here are for the most part rooted in tension, alarm and pain. Therefore in some cases they have lost their interrogative form and are expressed as statements of refusal to participate.

2. Narrowing consciousness

An observer taking a cool look at the heated situation can clearly see that the issue is looked at from diverse points of view. No wonder there are different angles of approach to its various facets.

Some of these facets and angles are more or less familiar, others contain an element of discovery or surprise. Our reaction to the latter is usually in the strain of 'That wouldn't really have occurred to me, but you are right, it is indeed an aspect of the matter.' In the situation described the discoveries and surprises are concerned with non-economic aspects and angles of approach. The hard-boiled captains of industry of last century's social Darwinism would certainly not have been disturbed at all by them. Such 'robber barons' (as they were nicknamed even in their own time) only recognised hard commercial considerations. They would have felt uneasy and disconcerted in such a present-day situation, where the right of expression is given to a thing on which they enforced silence: the voice of conscience and responsibility. Not a voice which is usually emphatic and clear immediately in such situations, but more often a questioning voice. A voice which confronts us with what we call 'ethical' questions. I hope that I have now managed to make both comprehensible and acceptable what we mean when we talk about 'ethical' considerations and questions. I shall return to this point later, after first going into the other half of the twin theme of 'technology and ethics.'

3. Research and development

'Technology' is not so much a controversial expression as an extremely general one; it is nearly as vague a label as the item 'various' in an annual financial report. I think I shall be fairly comprehensible, and far quicker than was the case with 'ethics,' if I say that I define technology as the entire process of research and development, including, emphatically, the marketing of the resultant products or services. Especially those who watch this process as outsiders are inclined to forget that it is a fairly recent development – and, moreover, one which involves more than a simple enlargement of previous scales. Today's research and development is not merely an extension of yesterday's hushed-up study, or of the one-man laboratory in which so many important discoveries were made in the 19th century. In the first place, research and development has become more and more the work of large teams, though Nobel Prizes are invariably awarded to individuals or at most to twosomes.

Secondly, research in the sense of theoretical investigation has acquired far weightier importance. It is now the stage in which 'discoveries' are made which would previously have come to light only in the stage of practical experiments. And thirdly, under pressure of war and wartime conditions, research and development have become enmeshed in a tangle of strategic and commercial interests. When we speak of technology in the 1970s, therefore, we are speaking of a complex reality.

4. Emancipation

The theme being discussed is 'technology and ethics.' We are given to understand that there are points of contact between these two realities and we may thus ask what these presumed points of contact are.

This entire problem has a history – the effects of which are being felt up to the present time – which I have no wish to disregard. As long as technology (of course then only the distant forerunner of what we understand by technology today) was considered to be a Promethean attack on the sacrosanct domain of the Gods, there was no room for recognition of the problem. The sample applies to later periods in which the suspicion of black magic was cast on natural science and technique.

Present research and development are quite unthinkable without the preceding, lengthy and sometimes painful process of emancipation during which science and technology won an increasing degree of autonomy. In the 19th century they were described as neutral, objective and disinterested, and these adjectives became universally adopted. Not so long before World War II, a man as famous and influential as the protestant theologian, Karl Barth, attributed a considerable degree of autonomy to the sciences, stating in the same breath that he would appoint himself as 'watchman' to see that they did not encroach on the terrain of the Revelation.

The atomic bombs which ended World War II devastated not only Hiroshima and Nagasaki, but also established ideas on the autonomy, neutrality and disinterestedness of science and technology. Not at one stroke of course, but in the slower tempo of a growing awareness. For men of science it must have seemed as if they were once again being placed under guardianship: no longer that of religion, belief or the church but of the ethical concern for the continued existence of man and his world and for the maintenance of human dignity.

5. Current questions concerning research and development

I feel I may be excused from giving an extensive description of factual developments, and will confine myself to an outline of some major points.

An atomic bomb brought an inhuman war to an end; but removed from this news, the realization began to take shape that to end an inhuman war, use had been made of no less inhuman means. The atomic bomb disclosed an advance in human power achieved by science and technology; an advance which was to be acclaimed less and less as 'progress' and to be felt more and more as a threat.

In the fifties, research and development in the field of nuclear physics gave the major impetus to the emergence of 'survival ethics': the question of whether it is justifiable for research and development to generate a power which constitutes a threat to the bare existence of ourselves and succeeding generations. This is particularly pertinent because it is far from clear whether we can keep such a power sufficiently and effectively under control.

The latter point is directly connected with the previously mentioned trend in which research and development are no longer the responsibility of one person or a few individuals, known and answerable, but occur within a scarcely tangible and anonymous system of organizations.

Apart from nuclear physics, developments in the fields of biochemistry and pharmacy have contributed largely to the growth of ethical consciousness in regard to research and development.

The CIBA Foundation Congress with the motto 'Man and his future,' held in London in February 1963, evoked a long-sustained stream of protest against the disquieting and sometimes arrogantly presented possibilities for the manipulation of genes, the artificial creation of human life in vitro and so on, which were coming ever further within the reach of biochemical research and development. The relation between pharmaceutical research and development and industry and marketing first became apparent to the public through the deeply tragic affairs of the 'softenon babies': the birth of many misformed babies in 1964 in Germany, Belgium and the Netherlands, proved on investigation to be attributable to the use of softenon or thalidomide sleeping tablets by mothers during pregnancy.

During the last ten years far-reaching environmental questions have become a subject of increasing importance in the debate. The escape of poisonous gases in Seveso (Italy) and Tiel (the Netherlands) merely represents the recent peaks of an iceberg whose growth is usually more stealthy, just as the constant pollution and poisoning of the Rhine by French and German industry is a creeping danger to drinking-water supplies in the Netherlands.

Furthermore, the Western world, with its structure of prosperity based on research and development, is being more forcefully confronted with the fact that this structure is not an internal economic affair, but involves decisions which influence (in the most unfavourable sense of the word) the bare existence of the Third World. At the consecutive meetings of the United Nations' Conference on Trade and Development (UNCTAD) and at many other high-level institutes or congresses awareness of this fact is being expressed more and more urgently and threateningly.

6. Agoraphobia

Are we now, from these various angles of approach, occupied in subjecting science and technology to a new form of guardianship? 'Scientific licence' and 'academic licence' have, to say the least, to some extent liquidated themselves by allowing research and development to evolve into an anonymous system. Therefore this question should be whether the system is being subjected to guardianship. I consider it an extremely important question because it is a point of access to deeper insight into the reality of ethical considerations and problems.

On this point we often allow ourselves to be misled by appearances. At the personal level we experience the 'voice of our conscience' as confining and oppressive. Horrific expressions such as 'conscience-striken,' and 'pang' and 'twinges' of conscience have given expression to this experience for generations. It is as though our consciences affected our freedom of choice. And very often our responses are in a line with that experience: we try to compromise, to haggle, or to silence the voice of our consciences. In short, we resist our consciences. But what is it exactly that we are offering resistance to? It is a fact that we experience, not commonly but not exceptionally either, the voice of our consciences as a challenge and not as a threateningly or reprovingly raised finger. Our consciences draw us out of our moated homes, that is, away from the too-small world of private interests, the too-restricted view of reality, the weighing up at too short a term. It is a striking paradox that the beckoning perspective of more space, and therefore more freedom, may at first be felt as confining and stifling. We are not prepared to leave the safety and familiarity of our moated homes just like that. In fact our reactions are usually as grumpy and sluggish as if we had been woken up when we wanted to sleep our fill.

7. I am more than ...

If I may continue on the personal level, which is after all familiar to us all from our own experiences, I should like to point out that our consciences do not provide us with every possible aspect of a matter on which we are taking a decision (or evaluating afterwards). When faced with a specific decision I can ask myself: have I time for this, will it improve my finances, do I risk troubles with the boss, and a thousand other details.

Conscience lifts us up, as it were, to a higher level, from which we discover other pertinent considerations that have far more to do *with the persons we really are*. Only then can the realization strike us – sometimes forcibly – that we were previously busy identifying ourselves with our bank accounts, our jobs, our positions in society and so forth. As long as I am dwelling in that small world, a question like 'am I not depriving myself' inevitably means 'depriving my bank account, job, position in society.'

But actually *myself?* I had never really asked myself this question. In fact I *could* not ask it until I had let myself be drawn out of my moated castle and had become aware that I *am more than all these aspects*.

Our experiences can sometimes greatly reinforce this creative point of view. An instance is when, during World War II, farmers' horses were requisitioned in some areas. Alas, for some farmers this drastic breach in their lives led them to commit suicide; others were able to overcome the same dislocation of their lives because they did not view the loss of their horses as the loss of their entire person and existence.

People can indeed be crushed by an almost totally destructive situation – yet there are always some to be seen painfully struggling up out of the ruins, those who have realized that they themselves are *more* than what they have lost or what has been torn away from them. The challenge of the conscience is concerned with rising above only partial self-identification (he who lays claim to my belongings lays claim to me myself), which as such can put us on a false trail in regard to our true identities and – in conjunction with this – to what our true interests and achievements are.

8. Blinding specialization

The ethical problems around research and development are definitely not merely an enlarged edition of personal problems of conscience. They demand, as has been proved by experience, a far more complicated approach. Nevertheless, experiencing personal problems of conscience and reflecting on them offers us a serviceable approach to the macro-ethical problems. It is, for instance, quite clear that the latter, too, give rise to a feeling of oppression when we are confronted with them. This oppression, an apparent restriction of freedom, has very clear roots at the macro-level. There is no need for me to go into this development in detail. Far-reaching specialization and pigeon-holeing has taken place in the world of research and development so that it has become harder and harder for men of science to follow the scientific doings of their near neighbours, let alone their more distant colleagues. Not that this situation, inconceivable though it may be to an outsider, is a great burden to them. One gets used to it. And though one may be working on a fraction of a section of a field, one feels at home there. Yet at the same time there is considerable risk involved. Just as small nations with a glorious future behind them tend to show a laughable type of chauvinism, so a man of science, boxed up in his professional sector, may paradoxically arrive at statements purporting general validity. A painful case in mind is the remark made in regard to the atom bomb by Dr. Enrico Fermi, one of those involved in the Manhattan Project: 'After all, it's superb physics.' The atom bomb may be 'superb physics' at first glance, i.e. within the confined boundaries of a physicists' professional vision. But it is not superb physics in the final analysis, i.e. when all things, or at least many things, are considered. After all, it is a deadly threat to the survival of man and earth. The more so since, as we know thirty years after the first atomic bomb, the proliferation of nuclear weapons is becoming steadily harder to check. Just as the car is the common man's status symbol, so the nuclear weapon has developed into the status symbol of powerful and rising nations.

9. Apparent illumination

When the specialized man of science makes pronouncements which lie beyond the borders of his specialization, he does not in fact cross these borders but simply emphasizes their presence. In a previous field of work on 'Futures research' I had ample opportunity to observe this phenomenon.

I have already mentioned the CIBA Foundation Congress in 1963, where biologists, biochemists and related specialists were sometimes tempted to pronounce on 'Man and his future.' Many of the overall visions of the future have been woven on the same general loom: the society of the future is tacked on to one specific development in present-day society. This can be said of Daniel Bell's 'Post industrial society,' Z. Brzezinski's 'Technetronic society,' Steinbüchel's 'Programmierte Gesellschaft' (Programmed society), Dumazedier's 'Society of leisure' and so on.

The one-sidedness of these and similar visions of the future becomes apparent as soon as one examines the details of the leap from 'here and now' to 'there and then.' One writer ignores financial and economic considerations; another assumes that future society will come into being independently of any democratic process, and so on. The leap from a professional specialization to some future society is an interesting spectacle as a 'salto mortale.' But it is by no means a break-through of the narrowing consciousness to which specialization inevitably leads.

10. Visible impotence

When research and development are confronted – as they frequently are nowadays – with ethical problems from human fields such as war and peace, survival, environment, human dignity, social justice, solidarity and the Third World, they are actually being confronted with their limitations and therefore with their impotence. In the realm of governmental urban and regional planning, in which I have been able to immerse myself for some years, such impotence may be frequently encountered in reports drawn up for the government by scientific advisory committees. For instance, the question whether a second national airport in the Netherlands is necessary and desirable is answered in reports which contain the most up-to-date versions of cost-benefit analysis, but on the other hand leave entire issues – mainly those concerned with essential questions on livability and social change – undiscussed as 'memorandum items.'

The same picture is seen again and again, whether it has to do with the agricultural sector, in which economic returns and the rural population's share in prosperity must be increased, while at the same time further encroachment on environment and landscape must be prevented, or with the sector of industry and services, in which unemployment must be combatted or the level of employment maintained or extended, whereas this again may not occur at the expense of the environment or of our failing resources, and where, of course, the repercussions upon the Third World must not be forgotten.

11. Still, the show must go on

Technology and ethics is a rather abstract-sounding indication of an extremely urgent and topical complexity of problems. As already contended, this has in fact, and in no uncertain manner, cast research and development back on their own limitations and impotence. This is naturally a disconcerting and discouraging experience, which has not been sufficiently taken up as a challenge. However, to do this makes greater demands at the macro-level than at the personal level, as we shall consider further on. My impression is that this predominantly discouraging experience has here and there generated a tendency to let matters rest, to muddle on, or to indulge in marginal pottering. All under the quasi-realistic slogan that, whatever happens, the show must go on. It is doubtful whether this can be called a choice, but if so it is in any case a perilous and highly unrealistic choice.

12. Shocking information

It is, then, a choice connected with the nature of ethical considerations and problems. At the macro-level these are experienced more as disturbers of the peace and spoilsports than as besiegers of the confining borders of private interests, short-term policies and far-reaching specialization. However, they do not draw our eyes to some utopia but to an, in our eyes, deficient reality; deficient as a result of our specialization, professional blindness or other forms of blinkered consciousness. When Charles Dickens published his social novels in the previous century they produced many shock effects. People could not conceive that they had been able to be blind for so long to what was taking place practically under their noses. In our time we too are confronted, by way of imagination and feelings but naturally also by unemotional scientific analyses and reports, with realities – the consequences of atomic bombs, the impairment of environment and livability, the poverty, misery and injustice towards the Third World – which give us a shock. Reality is far greater and far more dogged by problems than we had thought or expected.

Does all this too immediately strike us as an ethical problem? Social novels – in our time also originating from the developing countries – and extensive scenarios about the impairment of the environment (for instance 'Ecocatastrophe' by Paul Ehrlich) are actually 'ethically burdened' from their conception. That is to say, they not only present dry material information, but also transmit the ethical disquiet of the author, or at any rate tend to do so. In scientific publications this is not the case, however, unless they are in the form of a more professional-scientific 'evaluation' or something of that nature, such as the Club of Rome Report. But in whatever form it may be, *realities* are brought to our notice and sooner or later they make an appeal to our conscience or our sense of responsibility. They stir up our feelings. They set something in motion. But what? And how?

13. Beyond science

Two things are both clear and certain here:
1. These realities do not do this automatically, and
2. they do not do it by means of any professional scientific process.
As to point 1: I react 'automatically' to an unexpected, strong light stimulance: instinctively, by shutting my eyes. But if I see a face and find it beautiful or kind, then a far more complicated process has taken place within me, in which a role may be played by past experience, my mood of the moment and many other things.

In the same way, certain realities only make an appeal to our conscience or sense of responsibility by way of complex routes. That is to say, we ourselves are more actively and intensively concerned than is the case with instinctive reactions, which occur almost independently of thought or feelings.

As to point 2: scientific research provides material which can appeal to our conscience or sense of responsibility, but the research itself is then no longer involved. The human sciences can clarify the conditions under which an ethical appeal is exerted by specific realities – mainly the personal attitude and the prevailing culture – but this does not mean that the occurrence of the appeal and our reactions to it are themselves human science realities. This is not a type of analysis or scientific research; it belongs to a different order of reality.

14. Ethical problems are are-problems

While it is true that ethical problems bear down upon us by way of sections or details – with which not only research and development, but also budgeting, programming, organization, etc. busy themselves – yet they are in no way partial-problems. They challenge us – expressed in everyday terms – to look beyond the ends of our noses. All our scientific categories and practical division of roles only enclose a part of the world in which we live and a number of the people that we are. The partial approach, ever more refined, is adequate to provide workability. At least up to the critical point when we are faced, in our work, with problems which demand far more of us. All we *have* in the form of know-how, experience, categories, roles and functions proves to fail us then. Ethical problems cast us back upon the bare existence of our world and of ourselves. Not all that our world and we ourselves *have*, not everything that one can do with these things, offers us sufficient support in responding to ethical problems. For such problems contain the challenge to break through to what man and world *are*. Ethical issues are (may I say, making reference to Stallaert's contribution to this collection) '*are-issues.*' They wish to cross the confining boundaries of having, to ask what the world is and who we are.

Responsible action is action in reply to what we and our world are.

15. World models only provide material

If ethical problems are to be called are-issues, we are left with some matters that need elucidation. The first one that I should like to draw attention to is the fact that are-issues, like ethical problems, cannot be solved with the aid of scientific methods such as the use of systems-analysis computer models (used, for instance by Meadows as a basis for the Club of Rome Report) or econometrical computer models (as developed by Tinbergen), by which details are given greater cohesion and can moreover be extrapolated to the future. This approach, aimed at greater cohesion, also fails to rise above the provision of 'material'; material that may result in an appeal to conscience and responsibility, and whereby a *technical* solution may well be proposed, but is nevertheless too short a vaulting pole to be able to reach the field of ethics. It is striking that the many 'world models' with which we have made acquaintance during the past years have impressed us by their highly specialized scientific level, and yet are disappointing, either because they have purposely been kept un-political, or because the ethical considerations they contain are 'edifying' rather than profound.

16. An ethical chat by the fire-side

It quite often happens – and this is the second point I should like to draw attention to – that ethical considerations and questions are presented with the best of intentions but poorly thought out, or have been insufficiently critically examined. It is, by way of comparison, as if an attempt were being made to solve complicated problems in human relationships solely by the use of proverbs, adages and 'knowledge of human nature.' But if ethical problems cannot be solved by professional scientific methods, is no solution possible at all? Are we fated to remain so shut up within the frontiers of professionalism that nothing is left to us but shallow wisdom, common sense, sympathy and all that? Or do we believe that having religious or philosophical principles is enough if it comes to the point? Yet how clumsily, uncritically, dogmatically or inflexibly do we actually handle such principles? In fact, why are we so unschooled and untrained, in comparison with our professional ability, when it comes to ethical problems?

17. Unschooled on wasteland

We may well call it tragic and even disastrous that our present-day world does so precious little to practise systematic cultivation of conscience and responsibility, although questions of conscience and responsibility are being fired at us from many fields of life with steadily greater urgency. This contribution on 'Technology and ethics,' which has materialized as a result of reflection on the present situation, has no choice but to end with an urgent appeal to those concerned not to shut themselves up within the confining borders of research and development! Rather let yourselves be challenged by the presence of so many urgent ethical problems in our world of today to train yourselves systematically in tackling ethical problems as these have been approached in different ways by the great thinkers of East and West from the time of antiquity. Let your systematic approach be a contemporary one, responding to the contemporary situation, and in the idiom of today's philosophy – for ethical issues are are-issues!

There can be no guarantee that this will lead to a general solution. But it would at least be promising if we were, at long last, to recommence systematic cultivation of this neglected level of reflection where so many decisions have come to grief or vanished into thin air.

X. THE BUSINESS CORPORATION AND HUMAN VALUES

Richard H. Viola

1. Introduction

The conference on decision-making in business has dealt with issues of the utmost importance – issues which are oriented partly on the ethics and morality of profit, public policy, trade unionism, private enterprise, and the social responsibility of business. These issues are so important that they are at the very heart of the problem of corporate survival in the Western world. It should be emphasized that the survival of the business corporation is essential to the well-being of society. In other words, the profit-making business corporation can make a contribution to society and to the quality of life in that society. But how will the business corporation ensure its survival? By maximizing profits? The answer, of course, as Professor Stallaert points out in his paper, is 'no.'

The survival of the business corporation is very much a matter of its role in modern society, demanding that it play an increasingly active part as a responsible member of that society. Responsibility goes beyond profit-making, providing employment or making products for sale to consumers. Business is one of the major institutions of a free society, and as such it must make a positive contribution to society like any other societal institution. But to be in a position to improve the society in which it operates, an institution must be viable and adaptable in order to survive and in order to continue making a contribution and not merely to 'take' like a parasite.

The questions now become 'How is the business corporation to survive?' and 'How is the business corporation to contribute to the quality of life in society?' These questions are interrelated; one cannot be considered independently of the other. It will be seen that the proposed answers are also interrelated.

2. The problem of organizational life

Western societies in this last quarter of the twentieth century are faced with an ever-growing number of problems. Among these are strained international relations, economic problems, crises of national leadership, and energy problems, to name just a few. The problem of work in these post-industrial societies is one of the major issues which must be addressed. Reference is made to the quality of working life, the decline of the Protestant work ethic and the meaning of work. These are problems faced by business corporations as well as government bureaucracies – indeed, by any 'work organization.' But since the conference is concerned with business the discussion will be confined to business organizations. These corporations are being faced increasingly with growing absenteeism, high staff turnovers, workshop sabotage and a general lack of job motivation. The quality of working life in complex industrial organizations is not very high. Many students at colleges and universities in the industrialized world find business boring, unethical, decadent, not attuned to the pressing societal problems of the 1970s, and a profession in which it is very difficult to find the kind of self-expression that promotes psychological growth and development.

But these are merely symptoms of more deeply rooted problems. Business decision makers are not getting to the essence of the problems because they have taken too narrow a view of the corporation. The view has been narrow in the sense that it largely excludes the human, moral and ethical aspects of the business enterprise. Furthermore, the social aspects have not been stressed sufficiently and those which have been emphasized may have been the wrong ones. The reason this has occurred lies in an inadequate approach to the study of organizations.

3. The need for a new organizational analysis

To view the organization as an open system is nothing new. This approach regards the organization as an organismic whole interacting with its environment. This interaction, however, means interdependence. The organization can impose constraints on its environment, and vice versa. What is lacking, however, is a more up-to-date way of conceptualizing the environment within which organizations operate. Up to now, most of the discussion regarding environment has been from an ecological point of view. The literature on 'business and society,' or on 'social issues in business' has largely dealt with problems of water pollution, air pollution and other ecological issues such as the ravaging of land through strip mining or saving forests from rapacious paper companies. These are crucial problems and it is not my intention to minimize their importance.

But the time has come when we must consider that the central factor in the environment is the human being. Man is the focal point of society. As a result, the new organizational analysis must focus on man's *values* as one of the most important elements affecting the environment. Modern organizational theory analyzes man's behavior within the context of the organizational system of which he is a member. Most of the literature on organizational behavior is concerned with the relationship between man and organization and how these two elements interact to affect one another. Our concern with human behavior has been primarily devoted to understanding man and organization in order to make modifications in the behavior of each so that they can become more compatible. The objective of this approach has been to try to create an organizational climate in which both man and organization achieve their goals and satisfy their needs.

This has been near-sighted approach because it does not seek to understand man as a *member of society*. We seek to understand man as a member of a business corporation as if that corporation existed in a vacuum. It does not. It operates in an environment. We must put man at the centre of that environment because it is pointless to talk about 'society' without reference to the fact that human beings make up society. We use the word society so carelessly that we tend to think of it as some amorphous, faceless mass. Society is people and these people work for a living. The organizational behavior approach of today fails to recognize sufficiently that man moves in and out of the organization as a member of society. He is not just a member of a corporation and his values are not shaped by the corporation alone. Man is a carrier of values. The worker's values are shaped by many factors *outside* the organization. They are molded by forces in society and these values are brought out in the organization. The managements of corporations, the decision-makers, must realize, then, that they are affected by human values.

4. Effects of decision makers' myopia

This near-sighted view of what the corporation is and what its environment is has had some negative effects on the management of the business corporation. Sophisticated decision-makers know how important efficiency and effectiveness are as managerial concepts. But business corporations cannot be effective or efficient if they do not understand the values held by their employees. Values influence and direct behavior and if the behavior of the employees is not conducive to their performing in a highly motivated manner, the consequences for the business are obvious.

It was stated earlier that business is one of the dominant institutions in the societies of the free world. The dominant ethos of a society will be reflected in the institutions of that society. Dr. Ramaer's paper alludes to this very nicely. For example, in communist societies there are no autonomous, profit-making, business corporations. The philosophical systems of these societies preclude the existence of a corporate enterprise system. Hence, the manner in which 'business' is conducted and the organizational vehicle by which it is carried are very much a result of the society or environment of the time. Business corporations must be in tune with and act in consonance with the society in which they operate. This means they must satisfy the needs of society or they will cease to exist as we now know them in the democratic world. But needs are not static and since they are based upon human values, organizations and their decision-makers must monitor shifts in values.

The human beings who work in business organization must be allowed full expression of their values *within* the context of the organization. Managers who are the decision-makers of business can no longer afford to ignore this point. Is the dominant ethos of our times the same as it was fifty years ago? Of course it is not. But the business corporation as a dominant societal institution was built upon a conceptual foundation that is now rather shaky. The old values that made up this foundation are now under fire. Business corporations must be adaptive to the new values that make up a new conceptual foundation – a new ethos. If they are not adaptive they may go the way of the dinosaurs.

Important questions are being asked of the decision-makers. How does one live an authentic existence in the corporate bureaucracy? Is it possible to become a fully functioning, autonomous individual in the face of the increasing institutionalization of most societies? And what of the deadening conformity required by this institutionalization? The over-organized technocracies have fashioned an ethic of materialism and an absolutism of rational efficiency that are being challenged by changing human values. What we are seeing is the emergence of values which are contradictory to the purest form of pragmatism. We are witnessing a shift in values in the direction of personalism with a corollary stress upon the primacy of the individual who is trying to discover his identity not only as a member of society but also as a member of a bureaucratic business organization.

The notion of man's nature as static is a peculiarly Western conception. This notion has been challenged by distinguished philosophers who have also questioned the relevance of man's relationship to his world, a world which includes the business corporation in which he is employed. Two eminent scholars whose ideas are worth mentioning here are Teilhard De Chardin, the Catholic philosopher-paleontologist, and Martin Buber, the great Jewish existentialist. Chardin says that man is only an embryo of what he will become and therefore he must maintain an unlimited openness to a limitless future. Buber suggests it is only in knowing other men and being known by them that man finds his identity. He argues that man's authentic existence comes into being only when a personal 'I' meets the personal 'Thou' and accepts the other as a human being. In other words man meets himself in meeting another.

These concepts represent certain values. Do these values have any place in business? The large, complex bureaucracies through which most of the free world's business is conducted sow the seeds of conflict between individuals inasmuch as they overemphasize competition, immediate results and profit. The only way in which Buber's ideas can be put into effect in business is if the decision-makers engage in more humanistic management. Can individuals who work in today's business corporations achieve their full potential as human beings? Can they be self-actualizing persons while at the same time working in organizations that were founded in a different time and on philosophical assumptions which may no longer be valid? The answer to these questions will only be affirmative if managers create organizational climates which are conducive to the employee becoming all that he is capable of becoming. To survive as responsible, humanistic organizations, business corporations will have to investigate the needs of their employees and the demands of the societies, both of which are based upon value systems. Decision-makers must engage in environmental surveillance and analysis. The improvement of the quality of life in business and therefore in society rests upon the manager's ability to monitor and understand the meaning of shifting values and the philosophical systems upon which they are based.

The conference has addressed the issue of decision-making in business. One of the major facets of decision-making is problem-solving and in this respect the business corporation is a problem-solving system. The role of decision-maker is perhaps the manager's most crucial. Therefore, the quality of his decisions are causal factors in the organization's success. This success has been defined in quantitative terms such as return on investments, share of the market, profitability, and increased sales. But a shift in society's values may result in changing definitions of organizational success. Future criteria may be related to how well the business corporation can maximize societal values. Business as an institution conceptually was not founded upon the necessity to meet broad social needs, as exemplified by shifting values. But business will have to change if its constituent organizations are to be effective, and effectiveness does not mean only decision-making to solve intra-organizational problems. Will business corporations address themselves to the important issue of satisfying newly defined needs?

With a redefinition of what organizational success means and what criteria are needed to measure this success, decision-makers will have to re-examine their managerial strategies. The point of departure for this must be an emphasis on the role of values and the importance of this role in the lives of the business corporation's employees. This is absolutely crucial because the failure of bureaucratic business organizations to satisfy higher order sociopsychological needs and to consider the importance of human values in the world of work has placed business at a crossroad. The most successful business organizations will increasingly be those which understand that the development of one's sense of self-esteem will be enhanced only if the decision-makers realize that man's values, attitudes, and beliefs which are shaped in society must be allowed their continued expression in the organization. Man's wholehearted participation in and true identification with the business corporation depends on no less than this.

5. The meaning of values

At this point it becomes most appropriate to examine the concept of values in a bit more depth in order that we may set some parameters for the definition as it is now used. Our concern thus far has been with the survival of business as a major institution in society and we are suggesting that an understanding of the linkage between human values and the business corporation contributes to that survival. How? Through the adaptation of business to the needs of its working members and society. Since we have used words such as 'survival' and 'adaptation,' the concept of 'life processes' is paramount. Values, then, as we employ the concept, are appropriately related to life and the quality of life. Accordingly, we must consider Kurt Baier's statement (1971, p. 40) that 'the value of something ... is the thing's capacity to confer a benefit on someone, to make a favorable difference to his life.' It is important to note that he calls values held by human beings 'dispositions to behave in certain ways.' Also implicit in the concept of values is the notion that they motivate an individual to expend time, energy or money in order to achieve given goals or objectives. If values change we can see, then, that behavior will change, as will the goals and objectives of one's behavior. Baier says that 'the values we already have now serve as the rational determinants of our choices. When we choose one course of action in preference to another we do so because we have reason to think that it, rather than the other course, will help us to realize at least some of our values' (p. 33).

We are therefore using the word values rather specifically. We are primarily concerned with values as *choices* that human beings make. An individual *perceives* that the choice he makes will enhance the quality of his existence. Two points must be made here. First, we use the word 'perceives' knowing full well that one's perception is a very personal and individual *view* of something. This view or percept is a product of one's past experience (which in itself is a very complex matter), attitudes, beliefs, education, and personality. As such, the perception may be considered by another to be distorted or inaccurate. But if this happens it is because the individual does not share the same 'world' as he who is doing the perceiving. Their realities are different. Secondly, when an individual makes a choice we must remember that there must be alternatives from which to choose. Otherwise it is not truly a choice; there must be alternatives from which the choice is made before we can legitimately call this choice a value.

Another important point that warrants emphasis is that when we use the quality-of-life concept we are doing so in an all-encompassing manner. This concept includes sociopsychological, ethical, moral, spiritual, and emotional aspects of life, as well as material ones. Finally, we can tie together the above elements and thereby see the linkage between the survival of the private business corporation and human values. This relationship or connection is through the medium of the quality of life. If the institution of business does not contribute to improving the quality of life in society (a matter with which human values are increasingly concerned) its very survival as we now know it is in danger.

6. A new perspective

The point of view taken by much of the modern organizational behavior literature is too narrow. It does not go far enough in its analysis of the problems of work in modern business corporations. And its approaches to resolving the problems are also too limited. Since the scope is narrow so too will be the analysis necessary to provide solutions. What is needed is a perspective which relates the organization to its environment by putting man in the role of the central actor in society. This perspective must also include the concept of societal forces which are changing man's values. Since man is a member of the corporation, business will be affected by social factors in its environment.

There are, of course, many forces at work in modern society which are impacting on human values and which therefore must be taken into account by business and its management. But all possible societal factors cannot be considered, owing to the constraints of time and space. We will address ourselves to two factors which we consider to be very important: (1) a new understanding of morality; and (2) technology. These will be analyzed with reference to their influence on human values and, specifically, how they are changing these values. In addition the implications for decision-making in business will be discussed.

7. A new understanding of morality

Morality must be thought of as a method for evaluating human conduct in terms of a system of ideas and practices of a given society, class or social group. These ideas and practices regulate interpersonal relationships and provide prescriptions for that type of behavior which will ensure society's survival. It is important to note that we are talking about principles of right or wrong conduct and that these principles are related to survival – survival not just in the physical sense but also in its psycho-social, emotional and spiritual senses.

7.1. An historical perspective

The Catholic View: Historically, the fountainhead from which flowed the principles and standards by which human behavior was adjudged right or wrong was the Judaeo-Christian ethic. This derived from the Bible, and as Western man entered the medieval period, the Catholic Church was the organization through which the Bible was taught. It was during this period that the church rose to its greatest ascendency. The church was one with society inasmuch as it provided a social framework which guided all human behavior. Although society was stratified into very distinct and rigid classes, all the activities of all its members were subject to the ultimate arbiter of daily life – the Church. These activities, mundane or important, were all to be directed toward eternal salvation. This was the common goal of the stratified society and the *raison d'etre* of religion.

What about economic activity? It was considered as merely one aspect of human behavior. As such, it was to conform to the same standards and principles of morality as any other human activity. This meant that economic activities were judged in accordance with their service to the be-all and end-all of human existence – eternal salvation. If accumulation of wealth was the goal of economic activities these activities were judged immoral and sinful by the church. The satisfaction of one's basic needs should limit economic activities. One should gain only the wages of one's labor – no more. Labor was not only necessary; it was honorable. Trade and finance were not good for the soul. They were disreputable activities. It was immoral to charge interest on money that was loaned just as it was to sell an article at a higher price than was paid for it. This behavior was immoral because it threatened the life of the spirit and therefore one's eternal salvation.

The philosophy that was dominant during the medieval period was scholasticism. Its most articulate spokesman was St. Thomas Aquinas, and from his writings one can see that the central life interest for man was service to God in this life in order that one could enjoy the beatific vision in the next. The quality of life was not a matter of economic well-being but rather of this service to God through service and even subservience to one's fellow man in a highly stratified class structure. If one's station in life meant subservience to those of a higher rank, so be it. One was serving God by performing a function or vocation which was appropriate to one's position in society. Doing the work of one's station in life, one's 'calling,' and receiving the just deserts (but no more) of that function was understood to be moral behavior. It enhanced the group's survival. But scholasticism certainly took a very dim view of economic affairs.

Calvinism: The doctrine of predestination, which was introduced by John Calvin, had very definite implications for the understanding of morality. It held that, regardless of how faithful to God's law one was or how many good works one engaged in, one was either among the 'elect' and foreordained for heaven or eternally damned. Man's eternal destiny was decided from his birth. No one could help an individual in his quest for eternal salvation. In contrast to Catholicism, there were no sacraments, no priests; man was utterly alone. This religious doctrine turned man toward individualism.

With reference to work and moral behavior, this meant that one was to labor at one's 'calling,' or specialty, in a very individualistic way but for the good of society. This was moral because it promoted society's survival. The organization of society was rational, with the concept of *utility* paramount. Work was carried out in an impersonal manner but had to be socially useful. This promoted the glory of God. Whether one was numbered among the elect or the damned obviously created anxiety in the people. This was the case in spite of the fact that all Calvinists were duty-bound to consider themselves among the elect. In this they were to be supremely self-confident. But how was one to achieve this self-confidence? The answer relates the doctrine of predestination to moral conduct.

The self-confidence was to come from completely losing oneself in work activities. Day-to-day working at a specialty, trade or function was related to the concept of the 'calling' and was also the only way the believer could relieve his anxiety regarding life hereafter. But there was another aspect to all this. Constant and purposeful work should have as its end-result tangible, objective and useful things. One's activities were to be fruitful. Behavior was to be rational and far removed from emotion and mysticism. This was the moral norm: to be self-controlled and disciplined. Life was to be systematic and well thought out. One's goals were to be achieved by organizing one's conduct in a calculated, thinking manner. And as an individual's work bore fruit in terms of observable, measurable results, then did not that person have empirical proof that he was among the elect? It was a sign of God's blessing. For did not God help those who helped themselves?

The concept that work should be the central life interest of the individual now evolved. This was the new ethic and at the core of Puritanism was the idea that one's calling was to have a spiritual aspect to it. One's specialty which was developed by applying one's skills enhanced one's own economic interests. In doing so the well-being of society was advanced. The division of labor was thus considered a divine plan. The justification for hard, continuous work as the most moral type of behavior was in the amount of private profit it generated. This in no way detracted from its value from a religious point of view. The following statement highlights the difference in the relationship between ethical conduct and human values that emerged from the medieval period to the Reformation:

If God shows you a way in which you may lawfully get more than in another way (without wrong to your soul or to any other), if you refuse this and choose the less gainful way, you cross one of the ends of your calling, and you refuse to be God's steward, and to accept his gifts and use them for him when he required it: you may labor to be rich for God, though not for the flesh and sin (Baxter, 1930).

This statement epitomizes the new ethic of work and economic activity. It gives us new criteria for judging moral and immoral behavior and it cloaks the pursuit of wealth with a moral and ethical sanction. Not only is the making of profit given spiritual blessing, it is now regarded as one's moral duty. The capitalistic ethos was on its way. The asceticism, rationality, orderliness and systematic planning that Calvinism espoused in terms of one's conduct produced a person of stern character. Capitalism began to flourish because this conduct, this behavior, was conducive to good business. It was also conducive to being religious. The bourgeois businessman symbolized a new class which considered riches attained for the glory of God to be a new morality which found official religious favor. As a result, the businessman was free to follow his economic interests wherever they led.

However, the riches thus gained were not to be spent on anything frivolous, ostentatious or pleasurable. Asceticism was the byword. Saving was ethical and moral. It is not hard to see how these attitudes, neatly intertwined into a socioreligious system, facilitated the accumulation of capital. Investment became a relatively easy matter. Calvin's doctrine of predestination condoned acquisitiveness. If one's calling did not result in riches this did not matter because the good and faithful laborer gained merit in hard work. It was his obligation and he had to work to justify himself and give proof of his 'election.' The attitude toward labor was that it was ethical and moral to pay low wages since the lowly worker was *obliged* to labor long and hard. This was his calling just as it was the calling of the bourgeois businessman to pursue and accumulate wealth. The types of values which surfaced were manifestations of the choices believers were told were good, ethical and moral.

And it is seen that Calvinism and its major offshoot, Puritanism, gave the Western industrialized world a religiocultural ethos which in turn provided a solid foundation for business. Adam Smith's discussion of the pin factory's specialization of labor is akin to Calvin's concept of the calling. The eighteenth century English Enlightenment was influential for capitalism and private enterprise because of its eloquent articulation of the concept of private property. In early twentieth century America, the scientific management movement was developing and it revolutionized the manner in which work was done. It also attacked problems of organization and administration. A detailed history of scientific management is not possible here. But the very important point must be made that these new attitudes toward work, organization and administration evolved from the classic concepts of morality as expressed in Calvinism. The business corporation and the practice of industrial management was built upon the Protestant ethic. The business corporation reflected the values of Western society and was in the vanguard in promoting the Protestant ethic's concepts of morality. As a result, there developed an intimate interrelationship between the corporation and society. Earlier it was pointed out that institutions exist only at the sufferance of the society in which they exist. Business not only existed – it flourished. It was in perfect harmony with societal values.

A Contemporary Perspective: Religious, political, business and academic institutions were under attack in the 1960s. The dissatisfaction with the institutions stemmed primarily from the fact that their clientele perceived them as overorganized, impersonal, and mechanistic. The individual was not at the center of these institutions. He was not valued as much as the system. The church, the corporation and the university had lost touch with society. They had lost their credibility. The leaders of these institutions spoke in the terms of classical morality but their words seemed empty, irrelevant, and hypocritical. Thinking persons began to question whether classic concepts of morality were any longer able to reconcile men to each other and to society's institutions. Moral confusion and nagging doubts culminated in a questioning, a searching, and an exploration for some answers to questions which were as old as recorded history.

Situation Ethics: One of the directions into which the searching took man was that of situationism. This is one of the 'new definitions of morality' that has evolved. It is an approach to behavior which challenges conventional wisdom. Fletcher (1966), the most articulate spokesman for this new morality, says:

The situationist enters into every decision-making situation fully armed with the ethical maxims of his community and its heritage, and he treats them with respect as illuminators of his problems. Just the same he is prepared in any situation to compromise them or *set them aside in the situation* if love seems better served by doing so (p. 36).

The key word in the new morality, as represented by situationism, is love. Fletcher uses the word in a very specific way by referring to 'agape.' It is Christian brotherly love in its highest manifestation and is characterized by an unselfish type of love which does not consider the benefits accruing to the giver or the cost to him. Agapeic love is not calculating. The merit of the receiver and the question of whether or not he deserves the love is of no concern. This is an ethically and morally challenging concept. In this new understanding of morality, agape is the only absolute. During the medieval period morality was equated to legalisms. Principles of right or wrong conduct were the rules and absolutes of Calvinism and Puritanism. Conduct was judged to be moral or immoral according to how well it conformed to law. There is no moral laxity in situation ethics. Consider St. Paul's statement that 'the written code kills, but the Spirit gives life' (II Cor. 3:6) and 'for the whole law is fulfilled in one word you shall love your neighbor as yourself' (Gal. 5:14).

The conference on 'Decision-making in business' is an appropriate place to discuss situationism because some very relevant questions can be asked about agapeic love. Is this love put into action? Is it the criterion for decision-making in business? The decision-maker in business can no longer afford to dismiss such questions as having no bearing on the work of business or as being relevant only to woolly-headed philosophy. The loss of credibility which business and other major societal institutions are experiencing is serious. The manager must become aware of changing human values which are reflective of new definitions of right and wrong conduct. These changing values will affect decision-makers in business inasmuch as their conduct will be judged according to new rules. So long as the only absolute, the 'law' of agapeic love, is obeyed, no condemnation of the decision-makers will be made. But is this the criterion used for decision-making? Before we attempt to answer this question let us explore in a bit more depth some of the most important concepts of situation ethics. There are four factors at work which Fletcher (1966) identifies as (1) pragmatism; (2) relativism; (3) positivism; and (4) personalism.

Pragmatism holds that whatever works is good. In relating this to conduct, ends or goals must be considered. 'Works for what?' is a relevant question if we are analyzing the concept that whatever works is good. When an individual is considering whether an act is moral or immoral, he has to identify that which he chooses or prefers. This raises the value issue. An individual can act pragmatically when he comprehends what it is he wants. His action is based upon facts.

As opposed to medieval thought, situationism recognizes that just because behavior is based upon law it is not necessarily ethical. Laws can be ambiguous. Paul Tillich (1963), one of the greatest Protestant theologians, says that 'every law is abstract in relation to the unique and totally concrete situation' (p. 47). Dr. Teulings said very much the same thing at the Nijenrode conference on Decision-making in business, when they discussed legislation and pluriformity. Thus, 'code' ethics do not necessarily result in moral behavior. It is important to note, however, that relativism cannot be taken to its extreme. Fletcher (1966) recognizes that this could result in amoral behavior. 'There must be an absolute norm of some kind if there is to be any true relativity' (p. 44). In situation ethics this absolute is love.

The concept of positivism, when considered in the theological sense, holds that faith in a divine being is not a completely rational process. There are boundaries to logic, and matters of faith and morals extend beyond these boundaries. They are matters which are not decided on the basis of deductive reasoning. As a result, moral behavior is a function of conscious choice. Since values are choices, we can say that moral values are decisions which, although they cannot be verified statistically, can certainly be justified. Moral values can be justified by the situation. Those who endorse the new morality are saying that values, since they are choices, are not matters of logic. Values like faith are matters of affirmation or commitment. In his fine book, *Ethics, Science, and Truth*, Dr. Stallaert has articulated this position very well. This new understanding of morality must find its way into the thinking of 'rational' managers and decision-makers in business. These executives are often too biased in favor of measurement, numbers and statistics. When managers believe that if everyone just had the 'facts' or the data they would all come to the same logical conclusion, they demonstrate a naïveté about human behavior. They do not understand how the perceptual mechanism operates within the human being and therefore they do not understand morality in its true sense.

Personalism is the fourth key concept of situation ethics that we must discuss. It puts the human being at the center of the stage in the drama of life. The new morality is person-centered, not rule-centered. It is oriented around the individual, not objects. Personalism holds that one's humanity is found through interpersonal relationships. Buber (1970) says that man truly becomes human only when the personal 'I' meets the personal 'Thou.' It is in this 'I-Thou' relationship that man meets himself. This is when he is really in possession of his self and is free in the best sense of the word. When man is free in this sense, he is responsible and can thus make people-centered decisions. This is not only a matter of morality but also of psychology. When an individual knows himself, understands himself and 'owns his feelings' he is better able to understand others. As a result, man's conduct is moral because it recognizes his obligations to his fellow man.

Those individuals who are committed to personalism perceive human beings as ends, not means. The epitome of immoral behavior is the exploitation by one human being of another. Much of the manipulation of people in institutional settings like the business corporation would not take place if managers made personalistic decisions. Of all the activities which managers carry out, decision-making is perhaps the most crucial. The complexity of decision-making in the corporation has reached new heights. Data relating to economics, engineering, finance, marketing, production, and research and development must all be integrated in deciding from alternative courses of action. However, there must be a personalistic perspective which recognizes that the *ultimate* level of integration in decision-making is at the human level. It is here that the person emerges as the unique, all-encompassing gestalt. With situation ethics, human values become paramount in decision-making. This is something managers should understand. The decision-maker's values affect his decisions. No amount of denial by managers can alter this fact. For a manager to insist that his decisions are free of values betrays either intellectual dishonesty or ignorance of human behavior. Neither can be condoned in the management of today's business corporations.

Along with the concept of personalism is the proposition that nothing else but love is intrinsically good. In other words the end or goal of values is the person and love is good because it is for the benefit of the person. Contrast this with the Calvinistic-Puritanical concept which considered love a measurable, quantifiable item. The wealth one possessed and the amount of capital one had accumulated were used in the Calvinistic-Puritanical doctrine to measure God's love for an individual. How long and how hard one worked at one's calling was calculated and used to measure an individual's state of grace. What we see here is a conception of love as property. Situation ethics, on the other hand, conceives of it as action-oriented and this brings a new definition to the concept and to the understanding of morality.

If love is to be action-oriented then the implication for decision-makers is clear: The end that must be sought is agapeic love and managers must, in making decisions, see to it that this type of love is served. In the field of organizational behavior we have been telling managers to understand their employees' motivation in order to improve their performance. The new morality now asks managers to understand their own motivation when they make decisions. They must ask themselves some hard questions regarding whether they are looking at the decision from their own vantage point and in an egoistic way. The era in Western society now is one in which the classic principles of scientific management are not equal to the task of moral decision-making. The organizational setting in which decisions are being made is now very complex. The simplistic prescriptions of scientific management did not account for the values of human beings in the organization, and decisions were made with managerial and organizational ends in mind. Now human ends must be served and the basis for this action is the realization of human values which are brought into the organization by its employees.

7.2. The Existential approach

A second approach to giving morality a new understanding is existentialism. It is not implied here that this is all that new. What is being suggested is that it offers different answers to the question 'what is man?' These answers are more in keeping with the post-industrial society in which we live. They are more relevant for our times. Existentialism cannot be called a philosophy and therefore should be described in terms of what it stands for. Friedman (1964) does this best when he says it is an all-encompassing attitude regarding human existence and represents:

... a reaction against the static, the abstract, the purely rational, the merely irrational, in favor of the dynamic and the concrete, personal involvement and 'engagement,' action, choice, and commitment, the distinction between 'authentic' and 'inauthentic' existence and the actual situation of the existential subject as the starting point of thought (pp. 3, 4).

This can be contrasted with the description of humanity in terms of equating the 'I' with the ability to reason. Descartes' *cogito ergo sum*, which was embraced by classic morality, is considered by many existentialists as an insufficient approach to man. It is lacking in its view because it does not consider the whole person. It does not view man from within, from the vantage point of the life he is living. The logical positivism and empiricism, to which many organizational decision-makers subscribe, view man as an instrument or an object. As we said earlier, they are very much enamored of statistical data and facts which can be proved. In their attempts to be 'rational' they view man-in-organization much in the same way a scientist would look at a microbe under a microscope – very detached.

One of the major differences between classic morality and the new morality lies in the concept of man's nature. It is important to note the contrast because of the relevance it has for decision-making in business. Classic morality held that man's nature was static. Good and evil were defined in terms of those things which were consonant or dissonant to the nature of man. But in existentialism man's nature is conceptualized as being in a dynamic state. That which is contrary to man's nature therefore cannot be static. What it means to be a man is a matter of individual choice, according to Jean-Paul Sartre. If this is so, then it is not possible for anything to be adverse to what man himself has chosen to be. An individual makes a decision regarding himself as he lives out his existence. Kierkegaard (see Friedman, 1964) says that every person has the power within him to realize an authentic existence so long as he does not choose to forfeit his individually. He talks of 'being that self which one truly is.' Man's deepest responsibility, then, is to choose his true self.

Man is striving to achieve this goal because to be other than himself spells psychological and existential trouble for him. Business corporations have not been in the vanguard of promoting this and other concepts discussed here because of the threat to them that is perceived to exist in this dangerous kind of thinking. Many of the institutions in our society have not encouraged discovery of the reality of self. It is not the stuff 'good team players' are made of. It is not what a good organization man is. He is to be what the organization wants him to be and the sanctions it can impose on the individual striving to achieve fully functioning status as a human being are well known to members of business bureaucracies. Here is a situation where an 'urge which is evident in all organic and human life' is, in all too many business corporations, being stifled. And to the extent that it is, business corporations and their managers who contribute to this stifling are behaving in an unethical and immoral manner.

One of the ways in which the individual can find his true self is in the I-Thou relationship mentioned earlier in this chapter. Buber, it will be recalled, said that it is in this I-Thou meeting that a person becomes conscious of himself as a unique individual, differentiated from other individuals. It is then that the individual shares in a reality and, Buber goes on to say, no sharing means no reality. Only when the I shares in reality is it an authentic being. The sharing comes through dialogue which seeks to establish a vital and dynamic relationship between two human beings. But it must be a genuine dialogue if there is to be sharing. Genuine dialogue means the individuals are truly listening to each other, see each other for what each is, and accepts each other in his own right. An individual in genuine dialogue perceives the other person in a non-judgmental, non-prejudicial way. The other person is always 'allowed to be.' This is moral behavior. In the business corporation is there an organizational climate wherein interpersonal relationships, communications, and encounters are genuinely dialogic? To the extent they are not, we have corporations whose members are inauthentic, underdeveloped persons.

There are further implications for morality in their existential attitude towards reality. The only reality for a person is his own and it is to this that one must relate in more than just a coldly rational or objective way. Logical-positivism and scientism say that the only way to gain knowledge is to be disinterested. Existentialism says man exists and this reality must encompass his total interest. To become endlessly concerned with one's existence is what is demanded of us morally. Since morality is related to one's existence it is concerned with human beings as individuals and is thus an internal idea. These are the criteria – internality, existence, and the process of becoming. When we use these terms, then, what is ethical and moral conduct cannot be judged by an outsider. Morality is realized by the existential subject who is always in the process of becoming a person and who is the only one who has a grasp of reality for him. Moral reality is *his* individual reality but it must always be in terms of the individual being conscious of himself as a person. It is imperative, therefore, that we understand the importance of the notion that each individual exists in the process of becoming a person. But, first, he must be free to become a truly human person. There is, as was stated earlier, the aspect of morality which deals with the immorality of those who prevent or stifle this process of becoming in human beings. This is a further understanding of the new morality, and it relates to Buber's concept of genuine dialogue wherein one allows the other to be.

This freedom to be means man can and must be responsible for his existence. Existentialism seeks to get man to take complete responsibility for his self, his being. It finds itself in opposition to the determinism and fatalism of Calvinistic thought which leaves man with feelings of helplessness and powerlessness. Man can be free existentially, and, once in the world, he does not have to float along, bobbing up and down, this way and that in the stream of life. Not if he chooses otherwise. There is no room for Calvinistic fatalism because man is obliged to be what he is. This is the sincerity inherent in existentialism. Man experiences himself in his existence, he recognizes himself, he is conscious of himself and determines himself. Man's consciousness is related to what value choices he makes.

At the outset of this chapter we said values were choices made because it was perceived by the person that these choices (as opposed to other alternatives) would enhance the quality of one's life. In the future we are going to see more choices aimed at understanding and finding one's true self. This is not just another exercise in fuzzy thinking which managers and decision-makers believe is typical in academia. It is eminently practical for mental health, for the management of business corporations, and for a fresh understanding of what it means to be moral. Why? Because man must be independent, insofar as his greatness is realized in his freedom to be his authentic self and not what somebody else wants him to be or what somebody in authority tries to manipulate him into being. This authenticity, however, starts with a subjectivity and self-inwardness which is the dynamic, living, and open center of man's existence. The reason this is not vague or woolly-headed is that intellect and will are very much involved in it. The intellect gives man his subjectivity through knowledge and information. Concern for one's fellow man or agapeic love is facilitated by free will. But the individual self has to be free and the person must be in possession of his self, for one cannot give what one does not possess.

It is rapidly becoming obvious that business corporations do not have a monopoly on values and beliefs. To be sure, they are monopolistic in many ways but business corporations do not hold a monopoly position when it comes to choices or preferences as to what it is man wants. Managers may feel they know what is best for their subordinates and for society but this may be a result of the fact that their vision of man is superficial. It is superficial because it was formed on the basis of legalism, obedience to authority, conformity and responsibility (to one's betters). These values were the outgrowth of a moral system of thought which is stunting man's growth as a self-actualizing person. It is not that the above concepts are 'wrong' when put into a different perspective. It is, rather, that they were propagated as the central meaning of life. Man's values are changing away from choosing these as things which will enhance the quality of his life. This is why a new mental revolution is called for in our business corporations. A more relevant view of man is needed by decision-makers in business, a view which is more appropriate for our times with all the turbulent sociocultural changes we are witnessing.

Under the traditional religious dogmas which spawned the classical concepts of morality, the will of the manager or anyone else in authority was seen as the will of God. Therefore, the subordinate in the business organization worked hard for the organization and its goals because it meant religious, social, and financial salvation. But today man has lost his belief in the institutions of society, not the least of which is business. There are other voices calling him and he is marching to the beat of another drum. And this beat is telling him he is less of a man when he denies his true self for that self which some corporation, some group, or some manager tells him he must be if he wants approval like a child from its parent. We said that man is at the center of the stage in society. He is its protagonist and as such he has a wide variety of interpersonal interactions which affect his beliefs, attitudes and values. The business corporation can no longer dictate what constitutes moral behavior, especially since, existentially, discovering one's true self and the necessary freedom and responsibility to do so is now a moral issue. So when a subordinate in today's business corporation does not respond in blind obedience to the demands of some arbitrary authority, he destroys two things: (1) the authoritarian concept of morality which does not allow autonomy for personal growth and development; (2) the subordinate's old self which is the first step to becoming a fully functioning person. A little more than 400 years ago Calvin gave man a new faith. Today, society's new understanding of morality is giving man a new faith. It is a faith grounded in man's need to live a genuine existence in which he has the freedom to find his authentic self. Business corporations and their decision-making managers will have to adapt to this new understanding of morality inasmuch as their organization structures, leadership, and job designs are conducive to the worker's growth and development as a person. This is what man values.

8. The age of technology and its impact on human values

Another major force at work in society which is having an impact on man's values is technology. It is closely related to the new understanding of morality because of the manner in which it has affected human relationships and the quality of life. In the discussion of Buber's concept of dialogue, the type addressed was one in which a person can find authenticity in his existence. This was what Buber called *genuine* dialogue. But there are other types of dialogue to which he refers. One of these is *technical* dialogue and it is characterized by individuals trying to understand some objective facts. They do not relate to each other as persons but only as sources of information or knowledge acquired through specialization in a technical function. One of the principal reasons for the prevalence of technical, as opposed to genuine, dialogue is the technological age in which society exists.

The term, technology, as used here, refers to the practical application of scientific knowledge. It is important to think of technology in its broadest sense. It should not be considered only in terms of machinery. The development of so-called wonder drugs, for example, must be considered as technological breakthroughs in chemistry and medicine. So too would be the development of open-heart surgery. The issue which must be addressed is the effect technology has had on the human condition. What impact is it having on society and the values of individuals in society? Certainly it is recognized that technology has been of tremendous benefit to mankind. Labor-saving devices and machinery have delivered man from much back-breaking work. Medical advancements have extended man's average life-span and technological improvements in the fields of communication and transportation have literally opened up new worlds to millions of people. The list could go on. No attempt is made here to deny the contributions to human welfare that technology has made. Also, it is not the purpose of this paper to advocate the end of technological development; this must continue. But it is precisely because Western societies will continue to advance technologically that some questions must be raised. These questions have to do not with technology *as* technology but to the *ends* to which technology is used.

The concern, then, is whether technology improves the quality of life or causes it to deteriorate. It must be remembered that the quality of life concept must be considered in an all-encompassing way and thus deal with man's total existence. This means going beyond economic considerations and including spiritual, emotional, socio-psychological, and cultural aspects of the quality of life. According to Deutsh (1967):

The relationship of science and values implies a double question: the mutual interrelation of science and the general values of a civilization; and the relationship of a specific state of scientific knowledge to the pursuit of specific purposes or policies. The first of these problems, the general relationship of science and value, and thus to some extent of truth and goodness, leads us close to the heart of every civilization within which it is examined. If conceived as mutually incompatible, science and values may frustrate and destroy each other, dragging their civilization towards stagnation or decline. As a mutually productive and creative partnership, science and values may succeed in strengthening each other's powers in a selfenhancing pattern of growth (p. 37).

Thus the critical nature of this matter can be seen. A society's very existence is at stake.

The problem can best be put in terms of feasibility vis-à-vis ethics. In the highly developed, technocratic societies of the Western world, people have become so enamored of 'progress' that they tend unthinkingly to equate technology with progress. This has led them to the point where it is said that if something is technologically feasible it should be done. Use of the word 'should' is normative. It has ethical implications and these are that technological progress is always good. This kind of thinking can be deleterious. And the problem is that this kind of thinking has insidiously found its way into the mentality of the people. In America it was decided to put men on the moon because it could be done. But should not the question be asked: What is the morality of spending huge sums of money to put men on the moon when over 10 percent of the population lives at or below the poverty level? Also, how has putting men on the moon – a most elegant technological feat – improved the quality of life of the vast majority of Americans?

So then, people must become more aware of the ramifications of being obsessed with technological accomplishments. The technocrats in society are not concerned with the socio-psychological consequences of their creations. They are specialists in computer systems, engineering, or in some branch of science. Their perception of reality is limited to their own fields. All outward phenomena and experiences are distorted to fit the categories of their own specializations. For them, technical solutions become ends in themselves. They are not concerned with moral, ethical, and philosophical issues because they have been trained to think that as scientists, their work should be value-free. Does not this aptly describe the scientists who developed the atom and hydrogen bombs?

Society has been conditioned to believe that all of man's problems can be solved by technical analysis. The result has been to put technology upon an altar at which the Western world kneels in reverent worship. Technology which, in its conception, was to be man's helper and just another tool in his tool kit is moving to become the master, and man the slave. In using technology to conquer nature, respect for nature and understanding of it has been lost. This is especially true of man's inability to understand his fellow man. All the technology developed since the dawn of recorded history has not materially increased workers' ability to better relate to one another as human beings. Indeed, it could be argued that man's inhumanity to man has reached a new height. Technology has helped man to develop more sophisticated ways of destroying himself. Technological innovation must proceed at a pace that is tempered by constant questioning as to whether a given step forward is improving the quality of life. Humanization of the technological revolution is critically imperative if social, psychological, and ecological considerations are to be placed on a plane of importance equal to technological considerations. This is the first step in freeing man from his enslavement to technology.

And this becomes very much a matter of education. More knowledge of the socio-psychological world is needed for the development of new cultural norms that can help society shake off the enslavement trap. Cultural advancement means a reemphasis in academic curricula of the classical foundations of Western civilization. Cultural heritage must be stressed and less emphasis placed upon the vocational aspects of education. Indeed, it is questionable whether students are really educated any more. They are trained in a narrow and functional specialization so they 'can take their place in society.' They become the technocrats spoken of earlier. They have rarely read any of the classics in the literature of Western civilization, do not understand history or art, and know little of the behavioral and political sciences.

But the very technology which is causing some of the problem alluded to earlier is also causing man's values to change. The young and more highly educated (in the true sense of the word) are very critical of science and technology because they are equated with weapon development, nuclear proliferation, industrial pollution, and tampering with life (as in genetic research). These two groups in society are rebelling against the depersonalization of the individual. They are objecting to the regimentation, standardization, and conformity which are the inevitable results of a uniform technological culture. Genuine dialogue becomes a rarity and technical dialogue becomes the norm. This is seen by the young and the educated as objectified and mechanized human interactions. Their values are prompting them to choose meaningful interpersonal interactions as they shift their values toward humanization and away from being robotized by technology.

In addition to stating the problem in terms of feasibility vis-à-vis ethics, there is a second way to express the problem of technology. This has to do with maximization of production. Reference is made here to a major tenet of the technological way of thinking: output should always be maximized. This has had a negative effect on industrialized society and the quality of life of its members. Corporations with this maxim in mind begin to manipulate their demand curves by creating the desire for their products through advertising. As a society places so much importance on production, it loses its humanistic perspective. The original reasons for production are forgotten – production is undertaken for its own sake. The result is a never-ending cycle in which means and ends are confused and production breeds the necessity for consumption which in turn necessitates more production. Huxley's 'Brave New World' is here. The 'efficient' living of Skinner's *Walden Two* is equated with the good life. But such cultures are dehumanizing. They impoverish the human spirit and stifle all that is spontaneous and creative in human life.

The technocrats who are managing the business corporations are also the decision-makers of their organizations. The emphasis they place on science and technology has also had implications for the quality of life *within* the corporation. As noted at the beginning of this chapter, workers in business organizations are also members of society. Therefore, what happens inside the business corporation invariably affects society at large. One of the most adverse effects of technology in the business corporation has been on work. When the industrial revolution introduced the concept of specialization of labor, the managers of business corporations saw this as a boon to mass production and efficiency. It was so at the outset, but as it evolved its effects on the human being on the job has been increasingly harmful.

The objective of the division of labor was to make work more efficient. Each task was broken down into its most simple elements and a worker only performed highly specialized functions. He would become very proficient if he worked in this way because he would repeat the same functions over and over again. This made sense to the decision-makers in business. They could mass produce products cheaply and efficiently and sell them at a price which mass markets could afford. But the automated assembly line took its toll on the worker. He became bored doing this repetitive, monotonous work. He saw no purpose in it as its meaninglessness increased in his eyes. As a result, he became alienated from his work. As the business corporation became larger and more complex he also felt a loss of individuality. Scientific management sought to increase efficiency by analyzing the work of the individual just as it had previously analyzed the work of machines. Indeed, scientific management perceived man as an adjunct to the machine he tended and thereby it came to be called the man-machine model of work. As man interfaced with machine he became merely an interchangeable part of this system.

As an interchangeable part, man became expendable. He was not viewed by the management of corporations as a completely human person because he did not do a complete, i.e., total job. Since he only performed partial, minute tasks, man was viewed as less than fully human. He was viewed as the function he performed. Man was equated with his work and since his work was partial, he was considered partial. It would be a mistake to think that this was only happening to the bluecollar worker. Office work is also specialized, repetitive, and mono-tonous. The white-collar worker became nothing more than a number on a punched card of a computer. This is even more serious because the industrialized societies are increasingly becoming *service* societies. In America well over half the labor force is engaged in service type work. This number will increase as the post-industrial societies become more automated, thereby needing fewer people for production. At any rate, as the complexities of organization increased and as workers were considered only in terms of the functions and services they performed, the alienation of individuals from work grew into an alienation from themselves and this drove them into an existential vacuum.

Work ties an individual to the mainstream of life. As one's work becomes meaningless, his life may not become meaningless but it certainly has a tendency to be affected and pulled in this direction. Work in highly technological societies offers very little opportunity for psychic income. It provides little opportunity for an individual to gain a heightened sense of self-esteem. How can one get a feeling of self-worth by soldering a wire to a printed circuit (for television sets) over and over again in the course of a day? Can a worker get any sense of achievement and self-fulfillment by attaching the lugs to the wheels of an automobile on the assembly line? If he puts four lugs on each of the two wheels (on one side of the car only – specialization!) he will at the end of the day have attached 4,200 lugs. This is on a typical automobile assembly line with an average speed of 70 cars per hour. This is technology at its worst. Many of the workers in American automobile plants take drugs and alcohol in order to cope with the deadening monotony of the work. Money is not a problem; they are paid well. So well in fact that many of the younger workers only work three or four days a week. That is all the time they can put in and still keep their sanity.

Technology which results in these feelings of helplessness and alienation is having an impact on human values. It is causing man to rebel against his being treated as a robot. He is making choices in the direction of self-actualization. This is a need latent in all human beings – a need to become all that man is capable of becoming. As this need is stifled by automated technology so are the opportunities human beings have for psychological growth and development. If business corporations' employees are emotionally and psychologically stunted they cannot possibly enjoy high quality lives. This, therefore, must affect society. It means, then, that the decision-makers in business have a responsibility to society to improve the welfare of society. This can be done by improving the quality of their employees' working lives. There is no lack of literature on the social responsibility of business. Much of it has dealt with the business corporation's pollution of air and water, its obligations to consumers, and its responsibility in the area of minority hiring. There is no intention of minimizing the importance of these issues.

What is proposed here, however, is a new perspective on corporate social responsibility. It is a perspective which views corporate responsibility from the vantage point of the individual's continued psychological growth and development as a fully functioning, self-actualizing, authentic person. The corporation and its decision-makers must understand that they have an obligation to the worker to create an organizational climate conducive to this self-fulfillment. Business corporations can no longer afford the luxury of thinking that because an individual has to work for a living he must leave his attitudes, values, and beliefs at the factory gate or office door and pick them up again on his way home. This kind of thinking by managers implies that man must stop being human during working hours. It is a very naïve way of thinking for a professional class which has always been noted for its realism.

Because business corporation employees are human, they bring to the work situation a set of needs which they want satisfied, at least to some degree. This is how their values are changing. Unlike their predecessors of a generation ago they have rising expectations for need satisfaction on the job. Merely being paid a good wage is no longer enough. The worker of today values good interpersonal relationships at work. This results from the need most human beings have for affiliation. The worker also values participation in the decision-making processes which affect his welfare. He knows he must live with decisions made by management and therefore he desires a voice in the process by which these decisions are made. Today's worker, contrary to what many managers may say, wants involvement in the organization. But opportunities for involvement must be made available to him. The desire for participation and involvement reflect value choices which are based upon the need human beings have for esteem and self-esteem. Finally, the worker values a meaningful job which is a complete module of work with an identifiable beginning and end, and over which he has some decision-making control. This is the kind of job which satisfies very strong human needs for achievement. If managers in business do not understand the need system their employees bring to the workplace the level of motivation will drop even further from the low level it currently has in most corporations.

Business corporations are losing more workers each day decision-makers refuse to acknowledge the part human values play in the lives of employees. The workers are not lost in the physical sense – they continue to come to work if they want a better material life. But they are lost to the corporation in a psychological sense. There is no commitment because their involvement has been precluded. The result is a singular lack of motivation and low productivity. Workers have taken 'early retirement' on their jobs. No business corporation can expect to stay in business indefinitely if this continues.

9. Conclusions

The managers of business corporations must take their place as leaders in society. They must become the new statesmen and take up their responsibility to improve the quality of life in society. This can be done by recognition of the fact that the business corporation is an *open* system. It does not exist in a vacuum and its interaction and interdependence with society mean that corporate managers must keep their fingers on the pulse of society in order that they can monitor the social forces which are at work affecting and changing human values. As managers of open systems, decision-makers in business must take some long overdue action if they want their organizations to survive as viable institutions in society.

The steps corporate management has to take revolve around what it must do within the corporation to make it a channel through which its employees can maneuver on their way to full expression of newly acquired values. Some of the managerial strategies which will accomplish this are:

1. A humanistic style of management in which interactions with employees are such as to maintain and enhance their feelings of self-worth and self-esteem in the light of their values.
2. Consultative management whereby employees can participate in the decision-making and goal-setting processes. This is especially crucial in situations where employees are asked to implement decisions and work toward goals and objectives which affect their well-being.
3. A complete rethinking of the meaning of work. This should result in a redesign of jobs so they are more expanded, complex, and meaningful. The objective of

this job enrichment should be heightened feelings of achievement and self-esteem when an employee engages in this kind of work.

4. A reconception of the corporation in terms of the *community*. This concept perceives the individual as a whole person as opposed to only a segmented one. It views the worker as an integral part of the life of the organization because the worker shares in that life. Viewing the corporation as a community abolishes the Weberian model of bureaucracy as the *sine qua non* of organizational structure. Community means redefining the kinds of interpersonal relationships which will take place in the corporation. It reminds us that organization structures are not bricks and mortar but nothing more than patterns of interpersonal interactions and relationships.

5. Implementation of a communication system that is characterized by openness and honesty. This is the kind of system in which there is mutual confidence and trust between managers and workers. Mutual interaction-influence processes are more possible in this type of system. Employees, in their interactions with managers, should be able to have an impact on them because the influence process works in the upward direction, not just from the top down as in the Weberian model.

These are important because they will put the business corporation more in tune with society. The business corporation no longer reflects the values of Western societies to the degree it did at the turn of the century. It is no longer in harmony with society. The manager cannot appeal to legalistic ethical and moral norms to elicit work from his employees. Nor can he rely on religious institutions, or their doctrines and dogmas, to tell his workers that his authority stems from divine origins and therefore he must be obeyed under pain of eternal damnation. Also, workers are not motivated by money alone; how much one earns has nothing to do with how moral one is. The manager must recognize what workers now value and the new principles of moral and ethical conduct that guide their behavior.

Man does not choose to be enslaved but values freedom and autonomy. If the worker does not choose to be imprisoned by outmoded concepts of ethics and morality, why should he want to be enslaved by technology? He does not, and his values are changing as he rebels against the tyranny of technology. Decision-makers in the technocracies which business corporations have become must put man before machines and human processes before technical processes.

In America we have a business corporation which has an advertising slogan that says: 'Today, something we do will touch your life.' Of course, they are referring to the products they manufacture. But it is a phrase that has a far more important connotation and it is a point that has been stressed in this chapter. The business corporations in the Western industrial societies touch the lives of millions of their employees. Add to this these employees' families who are invariably also affected and we get a picture of the tremendous influence the business corporation has upon society. This influence is power, and as such the business corporation has a very serious obligation to make a positive contribution to improving the quality of these millions upon millions of lives.

References

Baier, K., 1971, 'What is value? An analysis of the concept'. In K. Baier and N. Rescher (eds.) *Values and the future*. The Free Press, New York.

Baxter, R., 1930, 'Christian directory'. In M. Weber, *The protestant ethic and the spirit of capitalism*. Charles Scribner's Sons, New York.

Buber, M., 1970, *I and thou*. Walter Kaufmann (trans.) Scribner, New York.

Deutsh, K., 1967, 'Some problems of science and values'. In J. G. Burke (ed.) *The new technology and human values*. Wadsworth Publishing Company, New York.

Fletcher, J., 1966, *Situation ethics*. The Westminster Press, Philadelphia.

Friedman, M., 1964, *The worlds of existentialism*. Random House, New York.

Tillich, P., 1963, *Systematic theology*. Vol. III. University of Chicago Press, Chicago.

XI. ETHICS AND PROFIT

Luud M. Stallaert

1. The illusion of objectivity

The undeniable facts of life include birth and death, not as phenomena we observe neutrally as outsiders, but as facts to which we are most personally subjected. Does this mean, therefore, that they are only subjective? Certainly not in the sense of being uncertain, but certainly in the sense that we undergo them. Does this mean that a certainty exists of going deeper than objectivity? It is only within the scene that opens with birth and closes with death that we can speak of subjectivity or objectivity. There is a vantage point from which the subject can survey both objectivity and subjectivity. It is inescapably the point of view of a subject. There is nothing for the human being to see if he himself does not exist. Objectivity in the traditional scientific sense of the word in some way obviously presupposes this awareness. However, just as obviously it causes doubts in the areas of those who want to fight for undeniable objective truth and values – for is there any escape for the subject from being subjective?

1.1. The difference between being the subject and being subjective

What do we exactly mean? Let us hasten to disentangle the confusing situation in which we are in danger of losing our clarity of view. A fundamental distinction must be made between *being subjective* and *being the subject*. We can be subjective in our judgements about things. It means that obscurities, indistinctednesses, are implicit in our judgements owing to the incompleteness of our observations, unjustified jumping to conclusions, the use of emotion instead of clear observation. In all these cases some imperfection in the subject who is observing prevents him from reaching well-balanced, true and certain judgements. The judgement, as already stated, is inescapably the judgement of a subject, like any certainty is. However, the imperfection of subjectivity is not necessarily due to a subject's making observations but to the fact that his observations are imperfect.

This does not mean that the subject's observations are bound to be imperfect. An observation is imperfect when it is incomplete. The completeness of an observation is related to the purpose of the act of observation. If I, the observing subject, am content with the certain knowledge that there are three cigars in my cigar box, then the observation is indeed complete after I open the box and see that there are indeed three cigars. This certainty coincides with the truth of the fact.

I venture to use the word truth here. It anticipates the second part of the distinction which has to be clarified. Allow me to postpone it for a few moments. The example of the three cigars is extremely simple. If, for example, we want to observe a law of nature, or true love, or a moral law, it becomes much more difficult to complete our observation, because a law of nature, or true love, or a moral law, is not sensorially visible. The observation has to be completed with an act of (intellectual) understanding. It is undoubtedly the act of a subject and – to make the modern illusion about objectivity complete – such an act has been understood since ancient times as an act of assimilation, which is the opposite of being outside and neutral. This is not the place, I think, to go down to the roots of the act of understanding. We only have to answer the question of whether or not all human observation (understanding included) is doomed to be subjective, or whether there is any escape and hence what the criterion of escape is.

We can now pursue the second part of the statement: human observation, although it is observation by a subject, does not necessarily have to be subjective. But how can we really find this out? Would we actually have to dissociate ourselves from ourselves in order to become truly neutral, outside observers?

1.2. Being a subject and truth

The strange thing is that – even if we cannot (yet) see a way out – we can certainly indicate the criterion for this. We would have to dissociate ourselves from the subjects we are and identify ourselves with the truth. Is this possible?

Permit me to revert to my statement that it is only within the scene that opens with birth and closes with death that we can speak of making observations. This is indisputable. Why is this so assertive – as the statement of a subject? Does the subject dissociate himself from himself? In a way he does. The subject claims to express an aspect of truth vis-à-vis his own situation. Hence he claims to look upon himself from the vantage point of truth. This identification with truth finds its criterion in the perfection of the statement. It is not an opinion or a hypothesis that is expressed, but certainty; the observation is not perfect in the sense that we have a perfect knowledge of birth and death, but in the more superficial sense that there is no escape from its purport. In the period between birth and death, the human subject is a 'light' in which he is aware of existing phenomena. In the intensified period of explicit consciousness he is also aware of belonging to the phenomena himself. We have to go into the structure of this act of explicit awareness to solve our problem of subjectivity and truth.

1.3. The structure of 'I am'

Is it possible to speak of structural awareness? Is our awareness not indivisible? Awareness certainly means being one; it constitutes our 'I.' Yet within this unity we observe all kind of relations and tensions. As regards our question, there is a relation with being: 'I am.' The certainty of 'I am' is indisputable, for even if I seriously *do* question, I become aware of the fact that *I* am questioning and that to be able to question at all, this *I* has to be (as Aurelius Augustinus already observed in his famous '*si enim fallor sum*'). 'I am' is an entity; we cannot separate 'I' from 'am.' 'I' implies 'am' or, rather, 'am' implies 'I,' for 'I am' expresses that I belong to being; being does not belong to me; it is not subordinated to me. What also becomes clear in this observation is the tension existing between 'I' and 'being'; being transcends the limitations of my 'I.' Other I's and other kinds of phenomena exist. How does our awareness of them work? I can only become aware of 'me' belonging to 'being' and of my limitations in regard to other phenomena by transcending myself in my own being. This sounds rather strange (though it is not so strange if we consider that every moment of intellectual growth, for example the birth of new understanding, transcends our previous situation to some degree). How can I remain within myself and yet transcend myself? This possibility in the structure of 'I am' is given. It is given in the way I belong to being. In the fields of belonging there are many different ways and levels. For example, I have an orchard; it belongs to me. I have an arm; it belongs to me. My arm obviously belongs to me more closely than does a fruit tree. My belonging to being is so close that I belong to being in the way I myself *being*. Within this belonging and in virtue of it, my awareness of existing is immediate. 'Immediate' expresses a form of unity; the unity extends so far that to some extent I must speak of identity; 'To some extent'? Indeed, only to some extent.

I *am*, but I cannot reverse this statement. I cannot in the same full sense say '*being* belongs to *me*.' It is from my belonging to being that I am aware of the truth of my statement. It is from my very special unity with being that I am aware of my smallness relative to being. The way of my belonging to being in comparison with other phenomena is also special in that my belonging has the highly intense form of awareness. It makes our participation in being more explicit, more intense. Awareness is indeed a degree of intensity. It puts us in the 'light' of being aware of our own existence. Awareness itself is a degree of immediacy of contact ('immediate' meaning that there is no medium, no third object between me and my observation). Immediacy is a form of perfection. We have spoken of perfection with regard to birth and death. Perfection meant there was no escape from the statement; the statement is true. It will now be clear that the statement is true thanks to the immediacy of its participation – its unity – with being. I myself *am*. It is from my *being*, i.e. from my immediate and conscious participation in being, that I make the statement. In this way the statement is perfect in that there is no escape for me from making it once I have reached explicit awareness.

1.4. The criterion of immediate participation

It is due to my immediate (conscious) participation in being that I am aware of my smallness, of my limitations. My smallness and my limitations operate in the limitations of my vision and other senses; in my awareness I transcend my smallness to the awareness of being. Being is the all-embracing phenomenon. But because consciously (and immediately) I participate in being, I am aware of the other phenomena surrounding me, each in its own way also participating. It is indeed the structure implied in 'I am' that makes it clear that we are able to transcend 'ourselves.' What we transcend are the limitations of our senses and our restricted goals.

1.5. There is no 'outside a phenomenon'

And objectivity? It will be clear by now that it is *not* possible really to *be* outside a phenomenon. The phenomenon and I *are* both. This means we both participate in being and it is only within this participation and in virtue of it that we, the human beings, are able to contact the phenomena. What we in reality (have to) judge is their special qualities of *being*. Hence it is not as outsiders, but really as *insiders*, that we judge (aspects of) phenomena, as people who by reason of their belonging to being are inescapably interested in being. Being – to the extent of our understanding – is the measure of our judgements. The measure becomes deeper, more inclusive and more real, in accordance with our growth towards the heart of being. The path of our growth leads from understanding to understanding, not only the 'neutral' understanding of science, but the involved understanding of the human individual as he, in his 'I am,' is aware of and is confronted with the 'whole of being.' There is scientific growth and there is human growth. Scientific growth is important, for it can be useful; yet more important is human growth. However, although it is more necessary, in our cultural period we pay less attention to it. This is the field of ethics.

2. The meaning of ethics

2.1. The full acceptance of our condition

Ethics is nothing but the full acceptation of our most real human condition. This condition is not related to business, or politics, or even to health, but to being. The very fact that many thinkers deny the possibility of knowing the relation more deeply, or deny its sense, does not change its reality; on the contrary it is the recognition and, albeit somewhat negatively, the underlining of its undeniable reality.

2.2. A few points to be recognized

We have to go more deeply into the basic human condition to discover its sense more fully.

2.2.1. The one-sided activity of our senses

The first point to be recognized is that the awareness of being is not of a sensorial, but of an intellectual character. Our senses do not have a relation of awareness to being. To make this clear we can observe the way our eyes work. They are one-sided in their activity. The eye does not exist in its own activity of seeing. Our minds, however, are self-present and it is on this basis that women (or men) invented the mirror to turn the activity of the eye in order to let their eyes appear in the light of their own activity. But even in this case, owing to the one-sidedness of the activity of seeing, it is only the outside that appears. In the same way, our other senses and organs, our hearts, our stomachs, work on unaware of their own activity. The mind however, although incomplete in its self-presence, is present to itself. For this reason it is a source of questions. The most basic question is about its being. It is the question of the sense of the whole and of the meaning of 'my' being in it.

2.2.2. The mind's self-presence

Secondly, the self-presence of the mind is accompanied by its all-sidedness. The reason is that self-presence is a certain depth of being. Self-presence is inner. This is due to some indisputable closeness to being. The closeness is in the nature of immediate (conscious) participation in being. It is in virtue of this relation that we enquire into the sense of being. And not only this, but there is also no escape from enquiring into that sense. Please do not misunderstand me. We can try to forget these kinds of questions, but they arise from the very structure of our awareness, the structure of incomplete awareness-of-being.

As we have seen, it is by virtue of our participation in being that we are aware of our incompleteness. But it also is by virtue of this participation that we are aware of the universal inclusiveness of being. There is no phenomenon not belonging to being. Being is the background of our research in any field. But with this background the requirement of universality of our statements, of our discoveries, poses itself. Being is the 'place' in which we try to explain things. This is the case in which we make a simple, but true, statement. The statement implicitly asserts that its content is true before the whole of being. We go one step further when we discover a law of nature or of mind. The discovery of the law means the discovery of stability through past and future; the law shows – in accordance with its level and character – universality. It participates to some extent in the all-inclusiveness, the strict universality, of being. For this reason it is stable. We can build on it. The law is stable, not static. The law works; it always works in concrete situations. In this sense, human awareness asks questions about the force of its structure of (incomplete) awareness-of-being.

2.2.3. The confrontation with the whole of being

The human being, on the grounds of his awareness-of-being, is a confrontation with the whole of being. This confrontation can be – and often is – interpreted as primarily sensorial, since the confrontation is with the overwhelming expanse of the universe in time and space. But being, as we have already seen, is not an experience of our senses; it is an experience of our minds, and although this experience can, of course, take place at the level of our senses since our senses also belong to being, the experience is primarily intellectual. It is in our meeting with being that we consciously participate by the very structure of our awareness. This also means that being is not primarily of the nature of our senses. It is even deeper than our awareness, as the structure of our awareness explicitly manifests, for our awareness is the awareness-of-being. In our awareness we are vague, incomplete and dependent, aware of being. I must say here that the clearer the moment of awareness, the more explicit and the clearer the awareness of incompleteness and dependence is. Confrontation with the whole of being does not therefore mean confrontation with the sum of sensorially apparent phenomena. Our awareness of the universe (the whole) already by far exceeds the range of our senses, and makes it clear that the concept of this whole is the work of our mind. Mind alone is related to a whole, for it indicates a depth of being, a depth in which we are confronted with meaning. Related to being it is an ultimate question. Thus, when we have to say that human awareness is confronted with the whole of being this is primarily a confrontation with its meaning, not with its extension, or with something else of minor importance. It is a confrontation with meaning in which our own, most personal, lives are at stake.

2.3. Ethics, a choice

Ethics, we have said, is nothing but the full acceptation of our real human condition. This means that it is *the discovery of this condition, and on the basis of this discovery, that the choice of a line of conduct which is in harmony with it is made.* Here again some basic observations are needed.

2.3.1. The participation in being is existential

The participation of our awareness in being – this is of crucial importance – is existential; this means that it is not only, and not in the first place, on the level of our notions and concepts, but rather on the level of (our) being. This implies that a relation has to be established with being on its level. According to the existential level of this relationship it cannot adequately be expressed in terms of scientific concepts. The relation is deeper and more immediate than concepts can ever be. A concept at its best is an exact image of an aspect of reality. It is never reality itself. The deeper and more immediate relation to being is realized in a human attitude. Conscious as we are, we cannot escape from having an attitude. The attitude – according to the Latin background of the word – means that we tend to something. However, what we tend to can be a disregard of being because, while overlooking our most vital relationship, we try to realize something more superficial. But in this situation, too, there is no escape from the fields of being. There is only a deep inadequacy insofar as the very structure of our conscious being is concerned. By reason of this structure (of vague awareness of being) there is an existential hunger for realization of the meaning of being in our being. Again, this realization must not be understood in terms of notions or concepts, but in degrees of fulfillment, viz. in degrees of peace and happiness. Peace, as Aurelius Augustinus said, is the realization of harmony, not the complete harmony of happiness, but of basic harmony, which in the first place, of course, has to be found with being. This means that it must be realized in our awareness and as a state of this awareness.

2.3.2. The law of adequacy of method and goal

No goal can adequately be reached if we do not use an appropriate method. What is the adequate method to reach being? To begin with, no method of scientific discovery will suffice. The obvious reasons for this are that scientific method is inevitably a specialisation developed to deal with a limited field of reality. It tries to regard its objective from the viewpoint of the impartial outsider. But being is the whole and, since we belong to it in every detail and aspect of our being, it is totally impossible in reality to observe it from any impartial, outside point of view. Yet in scientific knowledge there is a point, an aspect, that can help us, for scientific methods have been developed to lead us to understanding. When we understand, we are no longer outside the phenomena. Such understanding is a process of assimilation. This means that in our own minds we reproduce the phenomena as far as we understand them. Hence understanding our solar system means that we reproduce in our own minds the way it functions. Similarly, we reproduce in our minds the functioning of an internal combustion engine, of a mathematical circle, of consumers' conduct in a market, etc. The reproduction is on the level of our concepts, that is to say on the level of images. Our real understanding in these cases is with the help and on the level of images. This is also the reason why we can be neutral and outside them to some extent, for we ourselves are at a deeper level, the level of being. As a next step, the understanding of a human being can help us, for there are indeed degrees of understanding. If we want to understand another human being we have to put ourselves in his place, as it were. The understanding, as in science, may again be somewhat neutral and from the viewpoint of outsiders. We are then content in our minds to reproduce an image of his situation in which we understand the way he suffered the injustice, the pain, the loss. There is a deeper way of putting ourselves in the other person's place by committing ourselves; we become one with him to a much higher degree. The level of our activity changes: it is no longer conceptual; it becomes existential. Justice, as we know, cannot adequately be dealt with by conceptual understanding; justice has to be done; it always has to be effected in a real and hence concrete situation. This conforms with being which is concrete in all its manifestations: in every hair of our heads, in every leaf of a tree, in every star, in every awareness. It is not a good thing to try to turn ourselves into outsiders from justice, because there is no neutrality in justice, as there is no possibility of being outsiders in the realms of being. Commitment to a cause of justice is existential; to some extent we identify ourselves with the person or persons in question, with the appeal to justice inherent in us. But identification is a form of unification. The existential name for it is love. Love at any level, sensorial or intellectual, is indeed an existential movement of unification. We also can reverse this statement: any movement for unification, at any level and to any degree, is a movement of love. This of course means that there is love in science and scientific understanding, for there is no scientific progress without interest. Interest is the spark, or the fire, of commitment, and every new understanding, albeit conceptual, is an assimilation with aspects of the field concerned. The most basic commitment in the field of our awareness-of-being is to become more completely aware of being. And as this movement is existential, it is the most basic love. By reason of dealing with being, it is capable of integrating all fields, for all fields belong to being. This is the very reason why a man or woman who tries to be just, tries to establish harmony. Justice cannot be partial. It must, at least in principle, be as universal as being.

2.3.3. The ethical attitude

But there is more. The fact of our awareness confronts us with being. The confrontation of course takes place within our relation with it. This means that being always is with us, even when we, in our preoccupations, are not with it. Ethics is nothing more than the movement to become explicitly aware of our relation with being. 'Becoming aware,' existential as it is, is the movement to be as close with being as being is with us, the movement of conscious identification. This means that ethics is an immediate and personal relation with being. This relation cannot be replaced by a formal set of rules or principles. It resides in an attitude of realising with the whole of our beings the being in us and in our world. This basic attitude is not, of course, contradictory to having rules. However, its importance is in the attitude and not the rules. Moreover, being, although we, in our awareness-of-being, immediately and consciously participate in it, completely transcends us in its deeper sense. This means that it is impossible for us to reach it. It also means that no concept and no image of our imagination can have the remotest resemblance to it. Our relation with it is in the centre of our conscious selves. It is in the depths of us where we are most hidden from ourselves. (Being is vague to us by reason of its depth and its inclusiveness). As we cannot reach being, being has to reach us. Our task is to let ourselves be reached. It means that we have to keep the centre of our conscious life where it really is in the being transcending us, and that we live out of it. To have our centre in being means that we transcend all our restricted occupations, that we dissociate ourselves from them, and 'listen' to being.

This listening is our way of identification with being; it is our deepest love. We call it prayer. When it reaches degrees of greater depth and intensity it becomes contemplation.

3. Goals of business

3.1. Profit-making and a hospital

We can regard business as something independent, as an abstract entity, and define it as an activity which has profit maximization as its goal. Business is of course a human activity; we cannot entirely disregard this; yet in our scientific conception we can look from the point of view of 'the' enterprise and arrive at a profit concept independent of the aims and purposes of the proprietors of the firm, of the personnel, the taxes, the stock-market. The great advantage of such a concept is, of course, that it can be used for all firms in the country, or even in the whole world. However, it is obviously a fairly high degree of abstraction, for a business enterprise represents the collaboration of human beings. This means that in reality the goal of the firm cannot be separated from the goals of those collaborating in it, at least not from the goals of those who have influence in the firm. This implies the existence of minor or major differences between the goals of business and the way profit must be defined. As is also clear from the papers of Van der Schroeff, Bouma, Limperg, Mey,[1] it is hard to make a clear distinction between the concept of profit and the intentions of the firm.

A hospital, an example which I have come across more than once, exists without a profit motive. But is this a fair comparison? 'The' hospital does not indeed need to make profit, provided the buildings, the equipment, the groups of variously qualified staff and the doctors are paid (for) and can go on being paid. The hospital is a non-profit organization. It just has as its goal helping those in need of help, human beings who are ill. But is this image really correct? Is it not just another abstract notion, in this case honouring an ancient ideal? Certainly the hospital is very useful. And certainly there will be hospitals in which the leading people have such pure, noble intentions. And of course one of the goals, although it is not profit-making, is the continuation of the organization. New buildings have to be put up, the hospital has to keep pace with world medical developments. But are not these elements of keeping pace with developments and the continuation of the organization also basic in business enterprises?

---

1. H. J. van der Schroeff, 'Bedrijfseconomische grondslagen van de winstbepaling' (1975); J. L. Bouma, *Leerboek der Bedrijfseconomie* (1968); J. L. Mey, *Theoretische Bedrijfseconomie I*; and Th. Limperg, as discussed by the above.

3.2. The meaning of profit

Allow me to examine on the other hand the more exact meaning of profit-making in business. Is profit-making essential if the organization's continuity is secured, if the putting up of new buildings is guaranteed, if new equipment can be bought to keep up with new developments, if all the personnel and staff can be paid, if the people providing the funds are satisfied? What then is the exact meaning of profit-making by 'the' enterprise?

To Limperg, profit is:

... the part of capital gains that is available for consumption.

To Van der Schroeff, profit is:

... the capital gains that can be paid [distributed].

Under the Dutch Income Tax Act, profit (rather differently, of course) is:

... the amount of the total gains obtained from the enterprise under any name and in any form.

To Bouma, profit (in a determined period) is:

... equal to the part of the increase in the equity during that period which can be withdrawn from the organized economy without harming its viability or endangering its continuity.

Bouma states more explicitly what Limperg's and Van der Schroeff's definitions imply.

To the *Inventory of Generally Accepted Accounting Principles for Business Enterprises*, by Paul Grady (Chapter II, ATB no. 2; American Institute of Certified Public Accountants, New York):

Income and profit involve net or partially net concepts and refer to amounts resulting from the deduction from revenues, or from operating revenues, of cost of goods sold, other expenses, and losses, or some of them. The terms are often used interchangeably and are generally preceded by an appropriate qualifying adjective or term such as 'gross,' 'operating,' 'net ... before income taxes,' and 'net.' The terms are also used in titles of statements showing results of operations, such as 'income statement' or 'statement of profit and loss,' or sometimes 'profit and loss account.'

To *Managerial Economics: Analysis and Cases*, by W. Warren Haynes and William R. Henry ('Profits: a Central Concept,' 1974, Business Publications, Dallas, Texas).:

Profit maximization is the central assumption in managerial economics. The reasons for the stress on profits are several. Profits are, after all, the one pervasive objective running through all business situations; other objectives are more a matter of personal taste or of social conditioning and are variable from firm to firm, society to society, and time to time. The survival of a firm depends upon its ability to earn profits. Profits are a measure of its success. Another reason for emphasizing profits has to do with convenience in analysis. It is easy to construct models based on the assumption of profit maximization; it is more difficult to build models based on a multiplicity of goals, especially when those goals are concerned with such unstable and relatively immeasurable factors as the desire to be 'fair,' the improvement of public relations, the maintenance of satisfactory relations with the community, the wish to perform a service to the community, the desire to increase one's personal influence and power, and so on.

It is therefore usual to proceed in the early analysis as though profits were the only goal. After the consequences of that assumption have been derived, it is possible to bring in other considerations. Economics has developed a systematic and sophisticated system of logic as long as the goal is one of profits; it becomes more awkward and cumbersome when it incorporates other objectives.

Is the kind of (extra) profit referred to by these economists (and those in Holland are leaders in their field) the very essence of 'the' enterprise? I would not deny that there are human beings with the vital goal of making as much money as they can. But we do not necessarily have to look to business to meet them. They can be found among doctors and politicians too. And in business they are to be found not only among the managers, but can also be discovered among less talented or lower paid employees; the goal of profit maximization is not achieved primarily by actually making money, but in the underlying mental attitudes. And there are many businessman of whom we cannot say that their goal is to maximize profit. They want to continue the enterprise, viz. the services it provides. They want to work for the social security of others. They also want to have a decent living. So what is the essential difference compared between these cases and that of a hospital?

3.3. The double abstraction

If we define the goal of business as profit-making, we are dealing with an abstraction in a double sense. We abstract 'the' enterprise as an individual entity and, insofar as we unavoidably have to deal with human activity, we abstract an aspect of business activity from all other business aspects by saying that profit-making is the essential point.

In almost the same way it is possible to abstract hospitals and say that money-making is their goal. The only essential difference I can discover is that hospitals are supposed to be non-profit-oriented organizations. And how precise is a supposition?

I am rather afraid that present-day professors of business administration – and not they alone – still derive their concepts of business enterprise from capitalism's initial stages.

3.4. Back to reality

There is no 'the' goal of business. In our day we are doing a gross injustice in defining many small enterprises as having profit-making as their goal whereas in reality the enterpreneur's goal is to survive in the social and political struggle and to make a decent living. We are doing a gross injustice in defining many big enterprises from the point of view of 'money-making' whereas the real goal of the managers is to produce useful goods and to guarantee a decent living to those who work in them and, hence, from viewpoint of 'the' organization have the unimpaired continuity of the firm in mind as their primary objective. 'The' organization then means those who work in it and, in a broader sense, those who in one way or another depend on it. We are doing a gross injustice when we take people who do have money-making as their primary objective as the example of what 'the' businessman is. We could do the same with 'the' union-leader, 'the' professor, 'the' politician, and so on.

In theory, we can generalize the human activity of doing business to 'the' firm. And we '*in abstracto*' can give it 'the' goal of 'making profit.' In reality, everyone collaborating in a firm has his personal goals. Most likely they are directed towards joy and advancement either alone or with his family. He needs the means to achieve his goals. Part of these means can be generalized and translated into general terms of money. For most workers and managers, therefore, earning money is probably only a sub-goal. The firm is the melting pot of personal sub-goals, its organization is the result of the particular abilities we put in, not based on completely free choice, but as valued in the broader framework of society (other desires and goals) by other persons. The result is not abstraction, but the specific product we (our organization) have to offer – this is not the moment to deal with the big influence of abstraction caused by science, in our organizations and products.

It is the specific collaboration of specific people with their personal goals and desires that makes it understandable that we, from person to person, have to take care of one another to some extent. Neither the abstract 'firm,' nor its goal of 'making profit' can explain to us why we have to do this. Nor can the abstract 'firm' or 'the' goal of making profit explain why we should look after our broader environment. These abstractions are more appropriate to explain why the collaborators in an organization create antitheses between them, for if profit-making is 'the' goal of both workers and managers, why should the workers or managers not take all the money they can or even more than they reasonably can, if their understanding of their own situation and its possibilities is incomplete enough?

3.5. The philosophy behind 'the' firm

There is an unexpressed philosophy behind the abstraction of 'the' firm and its goal of profit-making: it is the philosophy of egoism. There is little escape from this philosophy, because in 'the' firm there is no inner brake on the movement toward increased profit maximization. And as 'the' firm is an abstraction and as we have to translate this abstraction in terms of our specific situation, we, the workers of every industry (including hospitals and public service organizations) and of every department in industry have to fight for increased profits for our group. We have to do so because the goal of business is the maximization of profit. We have to do so as groups, not because we particularly like our colleagues in the department, but because we have to widen our individual egoism into group egoism in order to be strong. It is important to emphasize this. If we want to be strong we must be united. But here are other and better forms of unity than egoism.

4. Profit and ethics

4.1. The goal of harmony

The human being by reason of his awareness is confronted with meaning. Meaning deals with the whole of something. The ultimate meaning is of course related to the whole of being and to whole of us in it. And meaning, as we have seen, is not related to our senses but to our minds. Our senses are of course important when we reach peace or moments of happiness. But the very essence of this harmony is our awareness; it is a state of our awareness and no harmony will ultimately be acceptable if it is not the ultimate harmony with the whole of being. The reason for this, as we have seen, is to be found in the very structure of our awareness as the awareness-of-being. Harmony we also understand to be a form of unity. It is unity which produces joy and peace and happiness in us, the joy or happiness, for example, of two human beings when they find (or create) between themselves the personal and deep unity of love, the simple and deep joy of unification with a 'lovable' day of sunshine and beauty. But the deepest harmony of all is to be found in the conscious unity with being itself, the divine love of which all the founders of great religions speak.

4.2. Harmony and unity

Whether we are at the beginning or in the middle of life or close to its ultimate development, our attitude must be directed towards the meaningful centre of being. We deprive our life of its sense the very moment we change this basic direction and move it elsewhere, for example to profit-making. We take it away from the place where it belongs and in one way or another put it in our ego. We segregate ourselves from our possibility of complete harmony and create disunion. It means that once we go that way there is no halt; in principle we choose the war of all ego's against one another. Yet we cannot separate ourselves from being, nor can we completely forget the structure of our awareness. Thus we know that harmony is in unity and that in unity there is also strength. But we also know that we cannot reverse this last statement. Strength does not necessarily create unity, because there are many levels of strength. There is the strength of those who really love each other. Thus the unity of true friendship is strong. Strongest of all is the unity of those who do not want to abandon their orientation toward the centre of being at any price. They are undivided in themselves, but also in their inter-human unions, for their acting and thinking in union has its source in truth; they are in harmony with being, albeit this harmony is not yet complete. But we know of the strength that indicates unities from the outside, as we saw in Hungary and in Czechoslovakia, and as we also know of in democratic politics and in enterprises and trade unions and even in families. Real unions cannot be so created because the real union has to have its source in the conscious and free centre of the human being. This centre is deeper than that strength; it is more real, for it is closer to being.

4.3. Dictated union and free union

The dictated union is a union we do not care for. Care has its source in an awareness that is free to choose. Care is for what we (consciously) cherish. A certain wholeheartedness is needed. It means that in some way the whole of us participates in what we care for. But, although real care requires free will, there are deeper grounds from which our care arises. Real care creates cherished ties but it does so on the basis of ties already existing. For example, a girl truly in love cares for a young man. There is undeniably an element of free choice in this, yet this choice is innate in the mutual attraction between man and woman. Their free choise unifies them, with this tendency pre-existing at the sensory and mental level. Our deepest pre-existing ties are at the level of our awareness-of-being with being. We do not normally know the element of affection which comes from the side of being. Our freely chosen care in regard to being is the more or less wholehearted acceptation of the innate situation of which we have to some extent become explicitly aware. We discover that even the ability to care is innate. It is innate as a very real aspect of our awareness, as it is able to commit itself. This, as we largely understand, happens at the existential (and not only at the conceptual) level. Care itself is a discovering power. (It is the care of the painter that leads to the better painter. It is the love of beauty that enables us to discover deeper beauty. It is the love of truth that leads to the discovery of deeper truth. It is love and love alone that enables us to discover deeper love.) And as conscious discovery and understanding are forms of unification, the deeper existential discoveries of care create more intense and more explicit ties of love. Ties that make us understand (the divine) being as the source and the goal of our existence, of the ultimate harmony claimed by our awareness as it is gifted by its innate structure with the ability to attain this goal.

Real union comes from the inside, the disclosed relation with being is the source of its strength. All other relations having their source elsewhere are for the same reason, more or less superficial. They are untrue in the profound sense that they are unable to satisfy completely the deepest human need and, together with it, prevent wholehearted commitment. Therefore those who bring people together in such a union must always be apprehensive. Their apprehension itself is the manifestation of the structure of awareness.

4.4. The needle and the north

And profit? What I wanted to emphasize was that in the life of mankind there is an innate direction, due to its very structure, that has to be chosen in order to attain harmony and happiness. The human being has to direct himself towards the centre of being as it presents itself in the structure of his awareness. He has to orient himself towards it as the needle of a compass points to the north. It has to be his basic movement and goal. All other activities are therefore subordinated to this goal.

It is therefore a mere abstraction, an extreme simplification, to speak of profit maximization as the goal of business. And if we really mean what we say, it is – I am sorry to say – sheer stupidity. We are human beings, and we cannot have any goal other than to bring humanity to perfection. Doing business is part of this. Hence the criteria for what we must strive for in business and how we must strive for it must be sought in this more profound development.

The goal of business is to (produce and) exchange goods and services humanly. Taking a somewhat egocentric approach, 'humanly' implies that we must not overlook our need for a decent living. Its decency depends on and has to be measured by our human goal. In a pluriform world this means, in our collaboration with others who may interpret their goals rather differently from us, that the decency of living has to be decided mutually. Secondly, or better still primarily, humanly means that we never can, and never will, forget that we are dealing with human beings, that is to say with beings who have the same kind of goals as we have. These same goals make us humanly equal, even though our places in our organizations, our education, our talents, our everyday wants, may differ. All these points, however, are of subordinate importance. Whether we deal with those working with us in our enterprise, or with our customers, there are goals far greater than doing business. These goals must be considered and respected. This means that we must not be willing at any price to destroy or pollute the ecological balance of our planet, nor the more profound intellectual balance of those we are dealing with. On the contrary we will be guided – by reason of our own human goals – so as to help, stimulate, develop, clarify to the very best of our abilities.

We can of course say that the actual situation of business is really different. This may be true in very many ways. But this is no excuse. It leads only to the conclusion that the actual situation is simply wrong and that we cannot put off our obligation to change it.

It is totally unacceptable that business or economics should rule the world of human beings. It is totally unacceptable that technology and science and nature and tribes and nations should become the tools of profit maximization. We must start right away to put business back where it belongs, as a function, and a means for the true realization of human life. If we refuse to do this we shall fail to the same extent in the achievement of our own individual objectives.

XII. ETHICS AND THE SCIENCE OF DECISION-MAKING IN BUSINESS: A SPECIFICATION OF PERSPECTIVES

Stanley L. Jaki

1. Perspectives on science

The contribution of a historian and philosopher of science to a volume on decision-making in business is perhaps not so much an event as an incident that calls for explanation. It can be had by taking a brief look at standard textbooks on the science of business decision-making. Although there are many such textbooks, their contents do not differ too much. Most of them, like R. L. Ackhoff's *Scientific Methods: Optimizing Applied Research Decision,*[1] deal with technicalities and know-how, while a few, like C. W. Churchman's *Prediction and Optimal Decisions: Philosophical Issues of a Science of Values,*[2] survey the deeper background of the technique of decision-making in business.

As a former physicist I found no difficulty in seeing that the statistical methods gracing textbooks on business decision-making are a superstructure. The foundations are a concept of science which is usually offered with qualifications amounting to no more than lip-service. Such seems at any rate to be the case with the books of Ackoff and Churchman. This duality, a concept of science strongly endorsed and heavily relied upon, and its qualifications briefly mentioned, can give a historian-philosopher of science some second thoughts. Some of these, I think, might be profitably shared by those interested in more than a cursory reflection on the *science* underlying the know-how of decision making.

The concept of science endorsed by Ackoff and Churchman is essentially that advocated by logical positivists. Both Ackoff and Churchman stress the idea of empirical verifiability and the notion of control over data and processes as the essence of the concept of science underlying the science of decision-making in business. Commitment to this concept of science is fairly understandable in Ackoff's book which is aimed at giving the know-how. In the case of

1. New York: John Wiley and Sons, 1962. The book was written with the collaboration of S. K. Gupta and J. S. Minas.
2. Englewood Cliffs, N.J.: Prentice Hall, 1961.

Churchman's book, which mainly deals with ethics and its philosophy, the concept of science endorsed by him gives rise to questions which he does not entirely ignore but from which he always returns to the principle of empirical verifiability.

About the qualifications concerning the positivist concept of science little, though enough, is stated by both Ackoff and Churchman to give the philosopher of science a firm grasp of their strategy. Ackoff quotes with approval the words of one of his critics, Anatol Rapoport, who urged him to warn his readers in unmistakable terms that 'the scientific method is treated here from a certain point of view, where the point of departure is a "problem" defined in "what to do" terms.' Those other points of departure are subsumed by Rapoport under the term 'humanities.' In addition to science as an 'adjunct to technology,' there is also a science which is a 'branch of the humanities.' In other words, to quote Rapoport again, 'the frequently emphasized implications that science is power should be coupled with the equally important reminders that science is also wisdom, i.e., avoidance of self-deception rather than a gain of control.'[3] In Churchman's book this non-technological aspect of science becomes briefly visible in his references to decisions which scientists must make time and again, which are not based on the so-called scientific method. They are based rather on hunches, moments of inspiration, flashes of insight, subjective preferences, cultural conditioning and the like.

Although what Ackoff and Churchman say of the non-scientific aspects of science is not particularly deep, for a philosopher of science it bespeaks of problems that have prevented his relatively young profession from rapidly reaching the mental immobility of old age. Of course, ever since there have been scientists they have, in a sense, been philosophers; and since the rise of science it has been a typical temptation for philosophers to tie their philosophies to the science of the day. The philosophical strategies of Locke, Kant and J. S. Mill are classic examples. All of them were in a sense philosophers of science. Yet, the philosophy of science was not really a profession prior to the 1930's that saw the formation of the Vienna Circle and the subsequent impact of logical positivism. The main purpose of the Vienna Circle was the definite replacement of philosophy with a science which contained only empirically verifiable propositions. Such a science is interested only in control, not in explanations, which are considered by logical positivists as a branch of metaphysics and therefore nonsensical. For the logical positivists, problems mean confusion rather than a suggestion of deeper aspects of truth. As stated in the Manifesto of the Vienna Circle, for genuine, that is, positive knowledge, everything is on the surface in the

3. *Op. cit.*, pp. vii–viii.

clearly recognizable correlation of data.[4] If this is true, the search for knowledge grows old before it has lived its youth. So much about the background of the concept of science which is by and large endorsed by authors of textbooks on the science of decision-making in business.

As to the qualifications of this concept, briefly mentioned by the same authors, the historian of science cannot help recognizing in them the principal issues that has agitated his young profession almost from its inception. Although the first histories of science were written two hundred years ago, and although some monographs written on the history of science a hundred years ago are still indispensable because of their rich material, historians of science have been a distinct and noticeable profession for not more than a generation. That their profession is not only noticeable by its numbers but also distinct in its attitude is largely due to the influence of Alexandre Koyré. In 1961 at an international conference in Oxford he described the movement he sparked off as an effort to vindicate the notion of science as understanding against efforts (positivists and Marxists) to define science as practice and control.[5]

Historians of science inspired by Koyré accumulated a staggering amount of evidence that science is indeed understanding and not merely technology. The history of science is to an astonishing degree a history of concepts, and concepts are so many witnesses to the process of understanding. Concepts are, however, one thing; truth is another. For good reasons or bad, Koyré and his followers cared for concepts but not for truth, and as a result the main trend in the new historiography of science has been toward a notion of science in which the culturally relative and personalistic elements dominate.[6] There is of course a very good way in which one can say that science is a 'personal knowledge,' to recall the title of a classic book by Polanyi published in 1959.[7] But when all major

4. 'We strive for order and clarity, reject all dim vistas and fathomless depths, for in science there are no "depths," all is on the surface.' *Wissenschaftliche Weltauffassung. Der Wiener Kreis* (Veröffentlichungen des Vereines Ernst Mach; Artur Wolf Verlag: Wien, 1929), p. 15. The Manifesto was written on behalf of the Kreis by H. Hahn, O. Neurath and R. Carnap.
5. See *Scientific Change: Historical Studies in the Intellectual, Social and Technical Conditions for Scientific Discovery and Technical Invention, from Antiquity to the Present*. Symposium on the History of Science, University of Oxford 9–15 July 1961, edited by A. C. Crombie (New York: Basic Books, 1963), p. 852.
6. The self-destructive logic of this trend can best be seen in the books of the sociologist-psychologist L. S. Feuer (*The Scientific Intellectual: The Psychological and Sociological Origins of Modern Science* [New York: Basic Books, 1963] and *Einstein and the Generations of Science* [New York: Basic Books, 1974]) who claims that hedonism is the true mainspring of the scientific enterprise. The intellectually more respectable manifestations of the trend in question are discussed in Lecture Fifteen, 'Paradigms or Paradigm,' in my Gifford Lectures delivered at the University of Edinburgh 1974–75 and 1975–76 under the title, *The Road of Science and the Ways to God* (Chicago: University of Chicago Press; Edinburgh: Scottish Academic Press, 1978).
7. *Personal Knowledge: Towards a Post-Critical Philosophy* (Chicago: the University of Chicago Press, 1958), reprinted as a Harper Torchbook in 1964.

scientific advances are treated not as acquisitions of truth but as ultimately unfathomable psychological processes, like the emergence of a new Gestalt in the field of perception, then science is no longer what it has largely been believed to be, an objective road to objectively valid propositions. Nay, within a notion of science which eliminates objective truth, even the act of control deteriorates into a pragmatism steeped in the subjective.

While some historians of science have become increasingly self-satisfied about their success in finding a clue to science in its history, a clue which claimed that everything in science was largely subjective and that scientific ideas were like animal species locked up in a blind struggle for existence, many scientists and some philosophers of science took a very dim view of the situation. The scientists felt that the subjective image of science exercised an inhibitory effect on science students, who were therefore counselled against reading books containing that image.[8] As to the philosophers of science, mostly logical positivists, they saw their whole position undercut by the historicism of the new historiography of science. According to this historicism, science can in no way be considered as objective knowledge giving objective control over data and processes.

Yet the logical positivists had their own share in producing a state of affairs which was aptly expressed as 'science in flux,' the title of a very recent book.[9] Personally, I do not think that science is in flux. It is, rather, thinking about science that is in flux. Since it is the idea of science supported by logical positivists which dominates in books on decision-making in business, more attention should be paid to the kind of flux, if not muddle, which is a consequence of being consistent with the claim that the only valid knowledge is empirical verifiability and control.

This muddle has largely been the product of reductionism or the resolve to treat every problem in terms of physical method, the area where empirical verifiability and control seem to have an exclusive say and complete success. Mechanistic science was still in its infancy when Hobbes seized on its apparent simplicity as a model for social and economic legislation. That the result was a monster, a Leviathan, indicated what could become of future efforts along these lines. Newton had just died when a friend and admirer of his, John T. Desaguliers, offered on the accession of George II an allegorical poem on the

---

8. See S. G. Brush, 'Should the History of Science Be Rated X?' *Science* 183 (1974), pp. 1164–72.
9. J. Agassi, *Science in Flux* (Dordrecht: D. Reidel, 1975). The book, which is a collection of Agassi's essays owes its title to an essay of Agassi with the same title published in the Third Volume of *Boston Studies in the Philosophy of Science* (Dordrecht: D. Reidel, 1968), pp. 293–330, an essay that carries the subtitle: 'Footnotes to Popper,' an uncanny indication that Popper's criticism of logical positivism exchanged the definitive image of science as portrayed by logical positivists with an image with no fixed features.

Newtonian system of the world as the best model of government.[10] The idea of balance among the various branches of government as advocated by Montesquieu also owed much to Newtonian science. After Laplace showed that Newton's laws assured the stability of the solar system, political and economic theories based on physical science became the vogue of the day. The French Revolution owed much to such theories and inspired in turn many new ones. In his report to the legislative assembly on the reorganization of public instruction Condorcet declared that 'all errors in government and in society were based on philosophical errors which in turn are due to errors in natural science.'[11] What Condorcet said was actually an echo of a statement by Baron d'Holbach, who in 1770 published a completely mechanistic account of psychology, ethics, and sociology based on the principle that 'all errors of man are errors of physics.'[12]

Such a claim, even if not true, was at least expressive of the firm hope placed in the universal effectiveness of physical science and its quantitative method. Further evidence of that hope were attempts at quantitative evaluation of the question of happiness. Better known in this connection than Maupertuis' *Essai de philosophie morale*, published in 1749,[13] is Jeremy Bentham's 'felicific calculus,' which today is as much a source of amusement as is the formula which the Nobel-laureate chemist, W. Ostwald, gave early in this century. According to this formula $H = (V + U) \times (V - U) = V^2 - U^2$, that is, happiness ($H$) is the difference between the square of the energy (V) expended in accordance with our desires and the square of the energy (U) expended in defiance of our desires.[14]

There is nothing amusing in the grim reality which is the almost global implementation of Marx's claim made in the Preface of *Das Kapital* that his laws of economics and of history are as rigorous as the laws of physics.[15] One is,

10. *The Newtonian System of the World, the Best Model of Government: An Allegorical Poem* [etc.] (Westminster: Printed by A. Campbell, for J. Roberts, 1728).
11. *Esquisse d'un tableau historique des progrès de l'esprit humain* in *Oeuvres de Condorcet*, edited by A. C. O'Connor and M. F. Arago (Paris: Firmin Didot Frères, 1847), vol. 6, p. 223.
12. *Système de la nature ou Des loix du monde Physique et du monde Moral*, published according to its title page by M. Mirabaud in 1770 in London, but actually in Amsterdam. For quotation, see vol. 1, p. 19.
13. See *Oeuvres de Mr. de Maupertuis* (new ed.; Lyons: Jean-Marie Bruyset, 1756), vol. 1, pp. 165–270. Maupertuis identified the good with the sum of happy moments and the evil with the sum of unhappy times and believed to have found in this a quantitative scale on which the various ethical systems could be appraised with mathematical precision. For further details, see my *The Relevance of Physics* (Chicago: University of Chicago Press, 1966), p. 376.
14. As reported by H. Feigl in his 'Philosophical Tangents of Science,' in *Current Issues in the Philosophy of Science*, edited by H. Feigl and G. Maxwell (New York: Holt, Rinehart and Winston, 1961), p. 1.
15. See *Capital: A Critical Analysis of Capitalist Production*, translated from the third German edition by S. Moore and E. Aveling (New York: D. Appleton, 1889), pp. xvi–xvii and xxx–xxxii (author's preface to the first and second editions).

however, entitled to a furtive smile on seeing present-day economists derive for the variation of consumer-interest equations which happen to be, unknown to them, identical with equations for rocket trajectories.[16] The smile must be furtive because the decision made about ten years ago to give Nobel Prizes to economists clearly indicates that the quantification of business processes and problems of economics has reached a high level of sophistication and reliability. In fact, looking at some equations which earned Nobel Prizes for some economists, one is tempted to think that they provide for businessmen the same kind of verifiability and control which physicists derive from their equations.

The glitter of Nobel Prizes in economics does not, however, invalidate the old truth that all that glitters is not gold. The trend to reduce our intellectual grasp of business to quantities is indeed tainted by the glitter of reductionism. Its misleading light can easily be perceived from a case provided in the mid-1960's by a well-known American historian of the Civil War. According to his claim we shall never know the true causes of that war unless the complete voting record of all members of Congress is analysed by computers.[17] Such a claim, if true, would jeopardize all commonsense judgment, a consequence against which commonsense would rightly revolt. Clearly, exclusive quantitative treatment would lead us into pre-empting the obvious meaning and reality of things we are continually faced with. A humorous but telling illustration of this is the case of two Viennese housewives, one the owner of a cat, the other the owner of a five-pound piece of butter. As the story goes, one day the five-pound piece of butter disappeared. The housewife who lost the butter claimed that only the cat could come into her pantry while the owner of the cat claimed that cats don't eat butter. After having argued for some time, they decided to present their case to a Viennese rabbi renowned for his wisdom. The rabbi heard both sides, asked for a balance and for the cat. The cat was brought in and put on the balance. Its weight was found to be exactly five pounds. This means, the rabbi said, that we have the butter; then, scratching his head, he added with a sigh, but where is the cat?

Such is the disappearance of reality through the magic of quantities, or mathematics, which Ramsay MacDonald, best remembered as a British Prime Minister, once described as the 'attempt to clothe unreality in the garb of mathematical reality . . .'[18] This magic will appear to be a mere sleight of hand in

16. See the report of *The New York Times* (Dec. 29, 1965, p. 16, col. 1) of papers presented at the political-science section of the American Association for the Advancement of Science, Berkeley, 1965.

17. L. Benson in a lecture 'Quantification and History' given at Princeton University on May 11. 1967. For a general discussion of that trend, see *The Dimensions of Quantitative Research in History*, edited by W. O. Aydelotte, A. G. Bogue and R. W. Fogel (Princeton: Princeton University Press, 1972).

18. Quoted by D. Sarnoff, 'No Life Untouched,' *Saturday Review*, July 23, 1966, p. 22.

the measure in which one moves from plain physical reality toward the realm of human affairs studied by psychology, sociology, business and politics. Saying that the sun's mass is about 700 times that of the earth is saying hardly anything about the reality of the sun and the earth, but somehow we feel that this quantitative relation was not meant to be a substitute for the reality of the two celestial bodies. However, when one is faced with a differential equation which purports to express the ups and downs of Sino-Soviet relations,[19] one cannot help feeling that mathematical treatment deprives them of flesh and blood reality, or at least does great injustice to them.

That the quantitative method loses its relevance in the measure in which one moves from purely physical reality toward human reality, individual and social, is a theme developed in considerable detail in my book, *The Relevance of Physics*,[20] and this is, I presume, the reason why I was invited to the congress on decision-making in business. An essential part of human reality, individual and social, is the making of decisions, a reality all the further beyond the range of quantitative methods the closer one gets to the heart of the act of decision. Faced with that act, be it a decision about matters quantitative, logical positivists can only admit defeat. For them and for their concept of science, which is also that found in books on decision-making in business, there are only observable data, and their relationships. This is why logical positivists eliminate the act of discovery, which is intimately tied to decision, from the realm of rational discourse.[21] On the other hand, for the subjectivist interpretation of the history of science, which is very much focused on discoveries as decisions, its radical psychologism makes a fairly rational look at decisions impossible. Clearly, if decisions are to be understood, or rather if we are to have a concept of decision which is not positively misleading or simply meaningless, we must have a notion of science which avoids two extreme though very fashionable notions of science, one of which is fostered by logical positivism, the other by a subjectivist historicism.

2. Perspectives on decision-making

Books on decision-making in business give a very deficient picture of science largely because their authors overlook the fact that science is based on a long series of agonizing decisions which are not made on the basis of statistical

19. See report quoted in note 16.
20. See note 13.
21. The position is endorsed also by K. R. Popper whose best known book, *The Logic of Scientific Discovery* (New York: Basic Books, 1959) has therefore a title which is patently a misnomer.

estimates of success. Histories of science and, I presume, histories of business ventures as well, speak by and large only of successes. But long before the success or discovery comes, decisions have to be made. Twenty years before Newton published the *Principia*, he had made the decision to explore the question of gravity for both terrestrial and celestial phenomena, a decision which might have amounted to the sheer waste of a lifetime's work. Ten years before Einstein published his memoirs on general relativity, he had made the decision to devote all his energy to a question about which he had no positive scientific assurance of success. He, too, might have used up in vain the most creative years of his life. Indeed, his decision made in the early 1920's to devote the rest of his life to achieve the unification of electro-magnetism and gravitation failed to be crowned with success. One may also recall the case of Galileo who, around 1613 when he was already fifty, decided that tides were the proof of the earth's rotational and orbital motions. Much of his next twenty years were spent on working out his theory of tides, a theory which proved to be the great intellectual fiasco of his career.

History, as has been aptly said, is always written by the victors, who prefer to remember only their victories. This is why successes make up the prevailing image of science and technology. Decisions that were followed by success are fondly remembered although such decisions make up only a small percentage of all decisions. Faraday, certainly a great scientist, estimated that only 1/10 of one per cent of his conjectures, all so many small decisions, were fruitful in his scientific work. Such an estimate would certainly fit Charles Goodyear's many attempts to produce galvanized rubber. The story of the zipper would yield the same proportion between successful and unsuccessful designs. The same is true of efforts behind Xerox machines, Polaroid cameras, tubeless tires, ballpoint pens, electric bulbs, a list that could be continued indefinitely.

This is not to suggest that a typical businessman should resign himself to living with this proportion between failure and success. The point is that science is an endless chain of decisions, and unless the scientist is willing to make decisions, big and small, many of which will prove fruitless, he is not going to get anywhere. Scientists know this; only non-scientists would be shocked on hearing a great scientist declare: 'Our whole problem is to make the mistakes as fast as possible.'[22]

In that word 'problem' there lurks a sense of urgency to achieve, a sense which is keenly felt by all who want to produce in the most general sense of the word 'produce.' While political theorists can discuss for years on end the pros and cons

---

22. And, of course, to recognize them, as emphasized by J. A. Wheeler, 'A Septet of Sybils: Aids in the Search for Truth,' *American Scientist* 44 (1956), p. 360.

of a given policy, the political leader has no choice. He must act, he must make decisions because the next moment can be too late for successful action. Philosophers of science and historians of science can ruminate quietly on their wisdom provided by hindsight, the scientist must advance boldly. 'A good historian,' it was aptly remarked, 'is too much committed to the past to be either a creative political leader or a creative scientist. In science at least, if a man wishes to achieve greatness, he should follow the advice of William Blake: "Drive your cart and your plough over the bones of the dead".'[23] The history of business shows that the manner in which very successful businessmen drove their carts evidenced not only their sense of urgency but also marked their paths with corpses, corporate and individual. But let us not anticipate the perspectives of ethics.

The willingness of a scientist to make all his mistakes as fast as possible is not a reckless drive. Behind this willingness lies an assurance, a conviction that the drive will ultimately be crowned by success, because the interaction of all things, or the universe, embodies an objective order and rationality. Such is the universe of Copernicus, Galileo, Newton, and Einstein. They all knew that their assertion of it was a metaphysical commitment and not the reflection of empirical evidence. The readiness of scientists to make decisions and choices day after day will appear a mad gamble only in the absence of belief in a rational universe. A universe of chance is never the universe of scientists, but of heedless philosophers.

The idea of a universe of chance is generated by extreme starting points. One is sheer empiricism for which there are only disconnected, atomistic sensations, the other is the pure subjectivism of existentialism. A classic statement of the former position was given by Bertrand Russell: 'I think the universe is all spots and jumps, without unity, without continuity, without coherence and orderliness, or any of the other properties that governesses love ... Of unity, however vague, however tenuous, I see no evidence in modern science ... Order, unity and continuity are human inventions just as truly as are catalogues and encyclopedias.'[24] As to the existentialists, their notorious dislike of science is based on the intimate commitment of science to the idea of a coherent universe. That universe cannot be known by logical positivists, since the universe as such is not the object of sensory evidence. Historians of science stressing the subjective element in scientific thinking and decisions run the risk of ending up with the claim that the practice of science does not rigorously imply the existence of a rationally ordered universe.

23. As urged by F. J. Dyson, 'Mathematics in the Physical Sciences,' *Scientific American* 211 (Sept. 1964), p. 131.
24. *The Scientific Outlook* (New York: W. W. Norton, 1931), pp. 95 and 97.

Most philosophers and historians of science are bogged down today in either of two extremes. One is that we cannot have valid knowledge of a rationally ordered universe, the other is that we do not need such knowledge. In both cases, the decisions to be made by scientists will appear largely as a kind of gambling, a very superficial and dangerous view of science as a process of decision-making. In such a view, which is also the view of science endorsed by authors of books on decision-making in business, the act of decision is deprived of a solid foundation and coherence. The result is a vacuum which cries out to be filled. Existentialism tries to fill that vacuum by denying that it exists. This denial is not so much theoretical as practical: an invitation to find fulfilment in the art of decision as such with no respect to its coherence with other decisions. No wonder that existentialist philosophy did not give rise to a theory of business economics. Marxism fills the vacuum in question by its doctrine of the strict dependence of history, individual and social, on the tools of production. Decisions are transferred from the individual to the party, the infallible interpreter of that doctrine. Such is a strategy which from a distance, or rather from the outside, beckons as a haven free from trouble and full of security. From the inside, however, the condition of being freed from making decisions feels rather like being in a straitjacket. Clearly, a young man or woman who must yield to the party the decision as to what professional career to embrace, will not be unwilling to look upon his or her condition as something akin to being in a straitjacket.

The vacuum created by the absence of a coherent basis for decision is for the Western world its very malaise, due to the steady erosion of its cultural heritage. The malaise is a crisis about decisions and was already in clear evidence a century ago. Kierkegaard was one of the earliest to note it. Bergson's philosophy, centered on the *élan vital*, was an effort to restore coherence to decision-making, not of course on the business level, but let us not forget that decision-making in business is merely a partial aspect of a much broader spectrum of the nature and problem of decision-making. William James's pragmatism was also an effort to give to decisions a basis and coherence. At times the suggested basis and coherence bore a curious similarity to traditional views. A good illustration of this is the phrase, 'the will to believe,' the title of a book by William James.[25]

Neither Bergson nor James nor other philosophers animated by similar concerns meant a return to the traditional Christian cultural heritage and matrix of the Western world. While in the early 19th century the shock of the French Revolution prompted a Romanticism which was strongly Christian in its

---

25. *The Will to Believe and Other Essays in Popular Philosophy* (New York: Longmans, Green & Co., 1897).

inspiration, the revival of interest in Christianity in the wake of World War II was much less vigorous. Yet in spite of their reluctance to counsel a return to Christianity, such interpreters of our times as Toynbee and Malraux recognized that the crisis of our culture is a religious crisis. According to Malraux, ours is the first culture in history which tries, though hardly with good prospects, to survive without a religious basis.

The lack of good prospects will not surprise those who consider the crisis from the viewpoint of man's ability to make decisions. It is this ability of man which tells him that he is free, and free to an astonishing degree, or rather to a terrifying degree, if one thinks of man's freedom to destroy mankind. Such a measure of freedom, such a far-reaching consequence of free human decisions, brings one face to face with questions of good, evil, and purpose on a cosmic level. The answer given to these questions is the answer which ultimately gives meaning to any and all decisions of man, including business decisions.

Personally I do not think that anything short of a positive reaffirmation of Christianity can be a good answer. History clearly shows that it was only a Western world steeped in Christianity that was capable of creating science, economy and business on a scale never witnessed before. This capability was a will to decide about a course of action which was deemed to be in consonance with man's position in nature as its God-appointed steward. To carry on with this course of action man needed a will corrected and strengthened by a transcendental vision which no philosophy or worldly wisdom could provide. It was only within a Christian matrix that man was able to live up to his capability of making decisions, which is the exclusive capability of an ethical animal.

Such is a hybrid definition, expressive of an unstable balance. Our times clearly show the balance tilting heavily toward the side which is animality. The result is not a course of action based on urges, but a confusion. Were man simply an animal, he would go on with the unerring instincts of animals, but since he is not, confusion and conflicts are the result of his urges. What makes this confusion truly so is that it is no longer deplored, as it should be. Modern man revels in the confusion of ethical norms, a point which takes us to the third main point of this paper, the specification of perspectives on ethics.

3. Perspectives on ethics

Whatever the willingness of a businessman to accept the claim that science is in flux and largely because of those personal factors at work in it which turn the human realm into flux, there will presumably be a general agreement about considering the science of ethics to be in flux. Ethical convictions, the subject matter of the science of ethics, are certainly in a state of flux. Long-traditional principles are rapidly losing their general appeal; indeed those maintaining them are instinctively being put on the defensive. Actually, there is no longer much arguing. Efforts to vindicate the exclusive correctness of a given set of ethical norms are being met with indifference if not incredulity. Reluctance to consider universally binding ethics is so instinctive as to turn up in the most unexpected context. For an illustration of this let me refer to a book by J. M. Ziman on science which carries the title, *Public Knowledge*, a title obviously aimed at Polanyi's *Personal Knowledge*. As Ziman correctly noted, a social or public consensus about the rationality of the universe was needed for the rise of science, a consensus which was displayed in ancient Greece, but even more so in medieval Christian Europe, the cradle of modern science. The failure of science to develop in other cultures can therefore be regarded as a result of widespread tolerance in those cultures of contradictory systems of explanation. This toleration, Ziman remarks, made the idea of a consensus about the rationality of nature 'as absurd to them, as the idea of absolute agreement on ethical principles would be to us.'[26]

Indeed in our times absolute agreement in ethics has already yielded to an agreement not to agree on anything concerning ethics. Concerning sexual mores, ethical relativism is now being written into law. Society is now forced by law not only to tolerate sexual behavior that until recently had been classified as aberrant, but society is forced to carry the financial burdens incurred by the consequences of aberrant sexual behavior. The removal of legal sanctions against incest, which has recently been proposed to the Swedish parliament, is a small but telling indication of the extent to which this process has already gone. The process is expressive of a complete ethical relativism which is supported by two philosophies. One is positivism, the other is evolutionism. According to positivism, only knowledge of facts is valid knowledge, while generalization about facts, especially metaphysical and ethical inferences from those generalizations, are without objective content and validity, and are therefore nonsensical. On such a basis it is impossible to have an ethical theory with a validity transcending the momentarily perceived or experienced facts. As to evolutionism, its principal proposition is that every form and state is purely transitory. Moreover, according to evolutionism, the succession of forms is ruled by a life-to-death struggle, a point which prompted one of the first reviewers of Darwin's *Origin of Species* to remark that Darwin's theory justified 'every cheating tradesman' and even a Napoleon[27] (happy days of 1860 when

---

26. *Public Knowledge: An Essay concerning the Social Dimension of Science* (Cambridge: University Press, 1968), p. 22.
27. See G. Himmelfarb, *Darwin and the Darwinian Revolution* (New York: W. W. Norton, 1968), p. 412.

Napoleon III exemplified the worst one could have in the way of dictatorship). That in evolutionary theory there was no room whatever for universally valid ethics was emphasized by Darwin's principal aid, T. H. Huxley. He warned against hanging 'moral flavor' around the doctrine of evolution and emphasized that invoking justice and compassion for the weak meant a standpoint radically opposite to the process of evolution which favored only the strong.[28] Evolution as an elimination of ethical perspectives was greeted with much enthusiasm by capitalism as well as by Marxism. The supression of weaker firms was described by John D. Rockefeller as the implementation of the law of nature.[29] Marx was so enthusiastic about Darwin's *Origin* that he asked its author to accept the dedication of the English translation of *Das Kapital*.[30]

A hundred years after Darwin and Marx, free enterprise and socialist economies are locked in a gigantic struggle for life with no consideration for ethics and ethical norms. Of course, capitalism and Marxism were not without some good effects for ethics. Their excesses and the justification of these excesses prompted such ethical reactions as Christian socialism, of which the classic documents are the papal encyclicals, Rerum novarum, Quadragesimo Anno and Populorum Progressio. The influence of Christian socialism as a system of ethics is today, however, in general decline. The kind of socialism which is today a leading force in Western Europe professes itself to be divorced from ethical philosophy, and there is no ethical philosophy either behind a capitalism which today is restrained by a wide range of social laws. These laws are becoming more and more pragmatic in character with all the threats to ethics inherent in pragmatism.

The intuitionist ethics which originated in our century with the *Principia ethica* of G. E. Moore in 1903 were largely a reaction against the degradation of ethics by pragmatism and evolutionism. This reaction did not achieve much in stemming the tide of the flux in which ethics or ethical philosophy has been for some time in the Western world. To begin with, Moore's claim that the notion of good is an absolutely valid notion verified by direct intuition was soon controverted by other intuitionists such as W. D. Ross and A. C. Ewing.[31] The

---

28. See his Romanes Lecture (1893) in his *Evolution and Ethics* (New York: D. Appleton, 1914), p. 80.

29. And of the law of God, nay of Christianity, as he claimed in an address given on Febraury 5, 1902, to the YMCA at Brown University. Somewhat inaccurate quotations from that speech were published in the same year in *Our Benevolent Feudalism* by W. J. Ghent (New York: The Macmillan Company, 1902), p. 29.

30. No sooner had Marx read the *Origin* than he informed Engels and Lasalle about its value for justifying class struggle. See Karl Marx and Frederick Engels, *Selected Correspondence 1846–1895* with explanatory notes by Dona Torr (New York: International Publishers, 1942), pp. 125–26.

31. See Chapter One, 'Intuitionism,' in *Contemporary Ethical Theories* by L. J. Brinkley (New York: Philosophical Library, 1961).

former saw in the notion of rightness the primary datum of ethics, whereas the latter claimed that the foundation of ethics lay in the notion of obligation. Universal agreement was of course in principle abdicated by the proponents of the emotive theory of ethics. According to this theory, moral statements are merely the expressions of feelings and have no more validity than the feelings themselves. One need not be a philosopher to see that on the basis of emotivism there is no moral obligation and that no realm of human experience reflects more of a state of flux than human emotions. Whatever ethics can be based on them can hardly be more than a total flux.

That ethical philosophy is in flux can also be gathered from the recent trend which is characterized by the resignation that a philosopher can at best search for good reasons to hold onto ethical theory. According to this position, it would be wholly presumptious for the ethical philosopher to emulate an Aristotle, a Spinoza, or a Kant who thought that it was not only possible to formulate the foundations of ethics, but that it was also possible to formulate a set of ethical norms binding all men always and everywhere.

From what has been said about the flux in which the theory of ethics finds itself, it would be tempting to conclude that a businessman is therefore completely at liberty to make any decision and that his sole constraints are those set by penal laws. Ethics would then be reduced to cleverness and stoicism, cleverness in eluding the law and stoicism in enduring its penalty. But the picture is not as void of sound ethics as it may appear. The flux of ethical theories and of ethical behavior is largely a surface phenomenon. Deep in man's heart there is a conviction that there is a sanctity to life, that the individual embodies a dignity which ought to be given unconditional respect. Tellingly enough, this conviction asserts itself most dramatically in the wake of flagrant violations committed against the dignity of the individual. The reaction against slavery and child labor bespeaks the steadiness of a moral conscience, and the revulsion against modern mass murders and genocides witnesses the depth of that same conscience. The recognition of the validity and binding character comes at times in the most unexpected contexts. As an example, let me refer to the Eddington lecture by James Conant, who on the one hand reduced the effective validity of Judeo-Christian ethics to childhood indoctrination, but at the same time also assigned general validity to some basic ethical principles in spite of what he claimed to be a universal inability to prove those principles rationally.[32]

A businessman concerned with the ethical dimensions of his decisions need not therefore fall prey to a sense of despair about being completely isolated. Even in this strongly amoral world of ours there is still enough sensitivity for ethical

---

32. *Scientific Principles and Moral Conduct* (Cambridge: University Press, 1967), pp. 33 and 37.

norms and duties. Nor need he feel distraught by the fact that the number of norms on which there is still tacit agreement is very small and that the norms are very generic. The whole history of morals, including Judeo-Christian morality, shows that efforts to specify basic moral principles can easily lead to a legalism and rigidity pre-empting the very notion of morality. This is particularly true in the fields of producing, distributing, and possessing material goods. As is well known, there is no tool that might not be abused, and it is almost impossible to evaluate exactly the amount of potential risk which is still within the bounds of morality. Indeed, the marginal risk which is tolerated in one area appears to be extremely narrow or extremely wide when applied in other areas. While for instance the 60,000 deaths and 1,000,000 grave injuries resulting each year from automobile accidents in the USA are readily tolerated by the American public, the increase of skin cancer from 1,200 to 24,000 in twenty years due to supersonic commercial flights is presented by many as ethically impermissible.

Such extrapolations are beset with great uncertainties, but such are precisely the cases which the businessman has to consider time and time again. He can handle them only with the statistical techniques of decision-making. Those techniques do not provide him with morality. They merely help him chart a course which produces the optimum economic benefit. Economic benefit is not, of course, equivalent to moral good. Indeed, it can turn into a rank exploitation of others, and such was indeed the case during the early phases of free enterprise. Social legislation now puts strong restraints on profit-making through free enterprise which, I believe, is the only practicable way of securing morality in business.[33] Other ways are either Utopistic or counterproductive. Undoubtedly, it would be desirable to live in a world in which all men, including businessmen, are guided by ethical altruism, but such a world exists only in Utopia. Whenever this ethical altruism is legislated, such as in a rigid socialist system, the common good suffers by the drastic reduction of the amount and quality of goods produced. It must not be forgotten that the optimum production of material goods is also a moral obligation.

Surely, man has a craving for economic security but it is also in man's nature to do something creative about his own material conditions. Any such economically creative act is bound to affect others, in fact, dislocate others in a cruel sense. The introduction of supermarkets resulted in the dislodging of many small shopkeepers, a fact that one can only regret and deplore. It is, however, unquestionable that supermarkets proved themselves to be indispensable for general well-being and that their introduction could not be slowed down to a rate at which all the harmful effects (dislodgement of others) could properly be

33. A chief representative of this position among economists is H. Margenthau.

provided for. Business profits always presuppose some innovation and every innovation implies inventiveness. Inventiveness in turn cannot be legislated and regimented. Any attempt to regiment inventiveness is bound to stifle it. Here, too, the business enterprise shows marked similarities with the scientific enterprise, which in a sense is an exercise of man's inventiveness.

Inventiveness flourishes only in an atmosphere of freedom and nobody expects scientists to forego new inventions only because inventions, like any tool, can be abused. One can bemoan the destructiveness of nuclear weapons but it should also be recognized that man's survival is largely based on the wide-scale installation of nuclear power plants. The controversy about nuclear power plants, which is very strong in the United States, shows not only, and very bluntly, the ethical relevance of business decisions, but also the impossibility of mathematical techniques to provide satisfactory answers. I doubt whether a recent and widely publicized article by Hans Bethe, a Nobel laureate, will convince ecologists and environmentalists.[34] Mathematics can only show the exceedingly small chances of the malfunctioning of nuclear devices but not the ethical obligation to tolerate a given level of risk, however small. Of course, this is not new. A hundred years ago T. H. Huxley had already aptly remarked: 'Mathematics may be compared to a mill of exquisite workmanship, which grinds you stuff in any degree of fineness, but nevertheless, what you get out depends on what you put in.' This is perfectly true of the relation of ethics to business. One's business decisions contain only as much ethical content and correctness as one puts into them. As to the success of decisions, let me continue with Huxley: 'and as the grandest mill in the world will not extract wheat flour from peascods, so pages of formulae will not get a definite result out of loose data.'[35] To tighten up one's data and to use ever better formulae is a condition of success, but not the key to it. The key is the willingness to make decisions and one's faith in them.

34. 'The Necessity of Fission Power,' *Scientific American* 234 (Jan. 1976), pp. 21–31.
35. 'Geological Reform' (1869) in *Lay Sermons, Addresses and Reviews* (5th ed.; London: Macmillan, 1874), p. 249.

XIII. INCORPORATING ETHICS IN BUSINESS DECISION-MAKING

R. Sybren Tijmstra

1. Introduction

This paper will endeavour to provide a general context for the papers and certain parts of the discussions in the session on 'Ethics' of the research seminar on 'Decision-Making in Business.' As already stated, this session was focused on the relationships between ethics and the decision-making processes in business. In the scientific study of decision-making in business, the topic of 'ethics and business,' or as it is sometimes called, 'business ethics' cannot be ignored in the world of today. When I say that it cannot be ignored in this era, this might suggest that this was possible in the past; the rest of this paper will make it clear that this conclusion would be wrong. However, owing to certain circumstances[1] the scientific study of decision-making in business has been centred on other topics, and the same applies to most of the public at large.

Before going into greater detail on the specific relationships between ethics and business decision-making, I shall first go somewhat further into decision-making in general and business situations in particular. In the second part of this paper, after discussing ethics generally, I will give some examples of business decisions and illustrate the ethical element in them. These examples will also make it clear that special attention should be given to the factor of 'social responsibility.' This factor is not of course as all-embracing as the factor of ethics but nevertheless contains some ethical elements.

In the third part, I should like to discuss the way in which social responsibility can be given concrete shape in laws and guidelines relating to business activities. In this part I hope to cast some light on specific problems in the domain of laws and more or less 'binding' guidelines intended to influence the conduct of multinational firms.

The last part of this paper will be focused on the incorporation of social responsibility in the objectives of firms. It will deal with the influence of ethics in

---

1. See section 3.3.

the purest sense of the word, i.e. the conduct of managers of firms, on decision-making. This article is not intended as a 'blue-print' of the way ethics (partly to be found in social responsibility) can (easily) be incorporated in business decision-making. If it forms a useful framework for discussion of the above subject I think it will have served its purpose.

2. Decision-making in business situations

2.1. Decision-making in general

By definition, decision-making in general concerns the process of choosing between alternatives. A choice is a question of pros and cons, implying that a number of factors have to be taken into account before a decision is made. At the end, making a decision can sometimes lead to the answer 'yes' or 'no,' and often to the setting of priorities. These are of course derived from something. The question is: what is the basis from which these priorities are derived? One could argue that, since in every decision-making process it is the people involved who make the decisions, the setting of priorities could ultimately be defined as a personal choice or the sum of a number of personal choices. This, however, suggests a freedom of choice which does not exist in reality. If it is defined as a personal choice, it must at least be said that it is made in a very restrictive framework, consisting for instance of the laws of the society the organisation operates in, or the organisation's formal or informal goals. Hence some of the alternatives that apparently exist in any decision-making process are already ruled out or made very unattractive by this restrictive framework. I do not think it advisable, therefore, to limit the discussion on ethics and decision-making to the pure form of the concept of 'ethics' but to include the concept of 'social responsibility.' I will revert to this 'social responsibility' concept and its relation with the concept of 'ethics' in the second part of this paper.

2.2. Decision-making in business: four categories

The decision-making process in business differs little from other kinds of decision-making,[2] as stated above. Here, too, the influence of society and the goals of the firm and the people working in it are of importance in this process.

---

2. See, for instance, M. A. M. de Wachter's paper, this volume.

The influence of both laws and goals have a restrictive character: some proposed alternatives are made impossible or at least will rank low on the list of priorities. I will revert to the meaning of this restrictive character later. For the purposes of discussion it may be helpful to divide decision-making processes in business into a number of categories; this will make it easier to set a framework for the papers of the 'ethical' session of the seminar and of the examples of decision-making given below. There are, of course, various ways of classifying the various kinds of decisions that have to be made.

The one I have chosen follows the chain of production: I distinguish four categories of policies which have to be decided upon again and again in business life:

1. Financial policies: these relate, for example, to acquisition of capital as an input factor or to the firm's taxation policy.
2. Social policies: that is to say, those concerning the factor of labour in the widest sense. They comprise not only the policy of hiring and firing but also working conditions, environmental aspects within the firm, and so on.
3. Technological policies: these include decisions on the firm's production methods.
4. Marketing policies: that is to say, selling the firm's products. It includes marketing and advertising, choosing products to be put on the market and getting orders.

This classification is in theory rigid, but in everyday business practice most decisions could be put in several of these categories at the same time. The main objective of the classification, however, is to subdivide business decisions for the next part of this paper so as to facilitate discussion of the possibilities of incorporating 'ethics' or 'social responsibility' in business decision-making. I think this needs some explanation, because at first sight one could maintain that the factor of 'ethics' is an all-embracing concept and therefore there is no point in subdividing decision-making in business into categories in order to make it easier to explain the influence of this all-embracing factor on such decision-making. In my opinion, however, this classification is justifiable because it will enable me to demonstrate that an 'ethical' decision in one category can have repercussions on another category which might be considered quite 'unethical.'[3] Therefore a decision which is purely 'ethical' in all respects will be hard to find in business or, for that matter, in most parts of society. Talking about ethics and business

3. See also the section 'Ethical problems are nearly always problems of choice' in C. H. I. E. M. Teulings' paper, this volume.

decision-making thus entails a discussion of the most ethical decision-making that seems to be feasible.

3. Ethics and social responsibility

3.1. Definition of ethics

In dealing in greater detail with ethics in business-decision situations, one immediately comes up against the problem of defining 'ethics.' Definitions of ethics vary from very general formulations such as 'the notion of good and wrong' or 'a set of moral principles or values' to more specific ones such as Stallaert's 'the full acceptation of our most real human condition.' Other definitions put more emphasis on dealing with one another i.e., social relations between people: this takes us more in the direction of group ethics. I do not think this is the place to start a semantic debate on the subject. I will therefore select one definition which to my mind reflects the important elements mentioned in other definitions. Ethics might be defined as 'the human striving for happiness, consisting of and/or leading to thoughts concerned with good and wrong.'

This definition of ethics, like every other, instantly gives rise to another problem: the roots from which ethics (and hence completion of this human happiness) can be derived. This could lead to endless debates with strong transcendental arguments in them. And this is what happened during much of the session on 'Ethics' of the congress on Decision-Making in Business. Probably everybody can agree on the thesis that ethics is a very personal thing, because it means a confrontation with the sense of life. Ethical awareness starts with the self-awareness of the human being.

3.2. Ethics and groups

Although one may agree that ethics is personal, it is possible for people to feel the same as far as ethics are concerned and this may lead to formalisation in ethical systems: to forms of ethics, with all the inherent risks of subjectivity and formalisation. Formalisation, for instance, is liable to become drab and superficial. During a certain period in history this resulted in the dominance of the Christian religion in at least part of the world, namely the Western industrialised world. Though the presentation of the present situation by Jaki is perhaps a bit exaggerated when he states: 'In our times absolute agreement in ethics has already yielded to an agreement not to agree on anything concerning ethics,'[4] it does indicate the changes that have taken place. And these changes have posed certain problems. If we take a closer look at ethical systems one aspect of them (and this is the systems aspect) is that they are bounded by time and place. If at a certain place and at a certain time there is no agreement on these rules, the problems of their incorporation in certain situations (in this case business situations) may increase considerably.

But let us go back for a moment to the personal nature of ethics. At the personal level no problems occur as long as the individual has no contact with other people: in these circumstances his concept of ethics is not threatened. But hermits have always been an exception, and in the world of today they are even becoming extinct. For most of their lifetimes individuals have to work in smaller or bigger groups. Troubles involving ethics then start at different levels. Firstly, if the organisation of the group is not based on a certain ethical *communis opinio*, this may cause a clash between the different individuals. Secondly, even if there is full agreement in the group on the content of ethics, the individuals the group consists of are probably members of other groups and the individual as a member of several groups may then have loyalty problems.

To summarize the argument once more: ethics can be defined as 'the human striving for happiness, consisting of and/or leading to thoughts concerned with good and wrong.' Ethics is a personal thing but concerns the whole of being. Individuals mostly work and live in smaller or bigger groups. During their entire lives and also at any time in their lives they are members of several groups at the same time. Most groups, with exceptions such as religious groups, do not unite on the basis of their members having the same ethical thoughts. Only if the society we live in had a *communis opinio* on ethics would we not have to bother about different ethical thoughts in the group within which we operate. In that case, our membership of several groups at the same time would not be a problem either. In todays' world however, even if we look at the different regions of the world separately, we see that there are divergent ideas on ethics. Which means that the 'ideal' situation referred to above is non-existent. The problem we are faced with is, therefore, the translation of the personal human striving for happiness into the group's striving for happiness, both in every group existing in society and also in bigger units and ultimately in society as a whole.

At this very moment this problem is more acute than ever before because in this era the interaction between the members of society and even between the different parts of the world has grown to tremendous proportions. Incidentally, I

4. See S. L. Jaki's paper, 'Ethics and the science of decision-making in business: a specification of perspectives,' this volume.

think this is, strangely enough, also one of the reasons why the emphasis on ethics in business decision-making studies has grown, as stated in the introduction.[5] An additional problem in formulating the group's striving for happiness is, of course, the transcendental basis of ethics.

3.3. Social responsibility

The extent of the problem we are faced with justifies in my view a closer look at elements in society where at least some (small) ethical aspects can be found. And one of these elements might be formulated as the 'social responsibility' concept. The purport of this concept seems at first sight a bit elusive, but can be developed pragmatically.[6]

It is formulated for instance in laws (at both national and international levels) and more or less binding guidelines. But it may also be of a very personal nature, as the term 'responsibility' indicates. In this very personal sense it entails some of the problems the term 'ethics' also presents. But it does not necessarily have a transcendental basis, which may be an advantage.

May I now illustrate with a few examples the fact that the ethical element (the striving for human happiness and so on) can be found in business decisions in the various categories mentioned above. At the same time, the tendency for an ethical decision in one category to have unethical repercussions in another will be substantiated.

3.4. Ethical elements in the various categories of business decisions

To start with an example from the financial category: In recent years there has been a lively debate on investments in South Africa. This problem arose not only at the level of firms wishing to invest in South Africa but also, for example, in regard to Dutch banks wanting to lend money for investment in that country. From a strictly financial point of view, there might be no ethical objections, and even the other three categories could have no ethical objections from the very limited viewpoint of the firm itself. However, this example already makes clear that the country or even the world the firm is working in may have a crucial

---

5. Other reasons might be technological progress (more about this in the rest of this paper) and the growth of prosperity in the Western world in recent decades, which has made it possible to concentrate not on the material aspects of life alone.
6. See also H. Schreuder, 'The social responsibility of business,' this volume.

influence on the judgement of the ethical justifiability of its acts. The argument in this case runs as follows: by investing in South Africa, that country's economy is stimulated or at least maintained; this means that the present political regime will be strengthened, which is ultimately tantamount to supporting the policy of apartheid. The opponents of apartheid describe this policy as detrimental to the human happiness of the black population. Therefore such an investment (or loan) should not be made in their opinion.

This example, however, brings us one level higher than that we have been concentrating on so far. For it refers not so much to 'social responsibility' at the level of the firm's home-country but to the world level. The specific problems that arise when a firm crosses frontiers will be treated in more detail below.

Another example, this time at the national level, of ethical problems that might arise in financial policies is a firm's policy regarding taxation. Laws of course regulate most of the domain of taxation, but as long as tax consultants still earn money, several different interpretations of these laws are apparently possible. Here again, an ethical argument might be advanced.

If one realizes that taxes are the main sources of income for the state to finance its expenditure on social services, etc., and given the assumption that the aim of such expenditure is at least to augment the human happiness of country's inhabitants, this would mean that any attempt to pay less tax than a most loyal interpretation of the tax laws would require is an unethical act because it puts at risk the human happiness of (some) people in the firm's country.

Of course, examples in the social category are the first many people think of when they talk about ethics and business. This is quite normal, because this category is the one where the most direct personal contacts are located and the most direct influence on the human striving for happiness occurs. Therefore, this was originally the field where most trade union activities were concentrated. As Hordijk indicated: in the course of recent years the trade unions (at least in the Netherlands) have moved their attention from this limited area to a more comprehensive approach.[7] An extreme example in this category of social policies is that of a firm wishing to fire some of its employees. The human happiness of these people is then most directly at stake.

As far as this group of policies is concerned this might seem an unethical act. But even within one category things may not be as clearly unethical as they seem at first sight. In the above case, take, for example, the fact that the management of the firm can prove that if they do not dismiss these employees they will have to dismiss the entire staff within a year because the firm would be bankrupt by that time. In this case, a temporary solution for some people (not to fire them) could

7. See A. Hordijk, 'Trade unionism and ethics,' this volume.

mean an unethical solution (firing the whole staff) for the firm's employees as a whole.

This category of social policies also includes decisions on co-determination, management policy or ownership: all kinds of decisions which formerly were hardly the subject of discussions between trade unions and management. In the sixties and seventies this has changed a lot.

Coming now to the category of technological policy decisions, we again meet with a group of business decisions which have recently attracted much attention as regards their ethical aspects. Much of the emphasis on 'ethical decisions in business' to my mind arises from ecological factors. Kreykamp's paper deals with the relation between techniques and ethics.[8] As Kreykamp points out, much attention in the past centered only the consequences of a given technological development. In the late sixties and in the seventies, however, attention has also focused on fundamental research.[9] In the technological category, examples are again abundant. To take one: a technological device is developed which makes it possible to produce a firm's products cheaper because fewer workers are needed. But the machine causes more pollution than the present production method. This is a good example of how the various categories are interwoven. Financially it may be ethical (the market position is greatly improved, which is good for the continuity of the firm); socially it may have unethical aspects (loss of jobs); technologically it may also be unethical (more pollution); while commercially it may be ethical again (cheaper products for the consumers).

Last but not least, a few words about the forth category: marketing policies. Teulings' paper gives some examples in which the ethical factor plays a major part, for instance marketing inefficient drugs or advertising luxury goods in underdeveloped countries.[10] I would like to add another example in this category, where we have to look not only at the firm's level or the country level but also at the world level. In a firm's order-getting policy, the following question might occur, 'Must we tender for the construction of a military port (or to put it more mildly, a harbour for the Navy) in, say, the Persian Gulf?' From the very strict viewpoint of the firm, this might again seem very attractive (high profits, plenty of jobs, and so on). But looked at from the ethical viewpoint at the world level such a tender may have many objectionable aspects (for example it would cause more tension and increase the danger of war in the region).

The entire discussion on 'hidden persuaders' (advertising and PR campaigns) is another example in this category of the ethical factor that has to be taken into account.

8. See A. Kreykamp, 'A reconnaissance into technology and ethics,' this volume.
9. See also M. A. M. de Wachter, 'Moral policy and public policy,' this volume.
10. See C. H. I. E. M. Teulings' 'Standards and values in the business enterprise,' this volume.

4. Incorporation of social responsibility in laws and guidelines

4.1. Social responsibility in national laws

The examples given above illustrate quite clearly that the ethical factor is ever-present in decision-making in business situations. How can we enhance the influence of this factor in this decision-making process? The environment the firm is working in already determines part of the answer; the laws of the country and international regulations provide certain minimum standards. The ethical factor becomes manifest in the form of social responsibility, which means that in actual fact these are minimum standards because there is no incorporation of ethics in the full, pure sense of the word. All participants at the session on 'Ethics' of the seminar at one time or another (in their papers and/or in the discussions) mentioned the role of laws in the incorporation of ethics in business decisions. They were also aware of the very limited function of laws in this context.[11] We must, however, realise, as Teulings[12] explicitly points out, that in the past many aspects of business were not a subject of concern to the legislator. Historically, laws with some influence on business decision-making started in most countries with social policies. Somewhat later, legislation on financial and commercial policies followed, whereas laws regarding technological policies are a fairly recent phenomenon. Hence in the course of the years legislation limiting business activities has been widely extended. As far as the Netherlands is concerned, we could speak of a complete 'structure of social-responsibility laws' regulating firms' actions to some extent at least. This 'structure' includes the ban on child labour, regulations on working hours and hiring and firing of personnel, the participation of labour in the decision-making process (work councils), regulations on financial reporting, non-aggressive sales methods, restrictions on advertising, anti-pollution regulations and many others. The influence of legislation on business decision-making has grown tremendously. But the law still tells us more what firms should not do than what they really ought to do, though this differs greatly from one category of decisions to another. For instance, at least in the Netherlands, much of the legislation on 'social' decision-

---

11. The paper by W. L. van Reijen, 'Power and legitimation,' adds to this limitation much more structural objections with regard to the legitimation of laws.
12. See C. H. I. E. M. Teulings, 'Standards and values in the business enterprise,' paragraph 2: 'The growing pluriformity of our value judgements,' this volume.

making is not of a restrictive nature only, while that concerned with the technological category of decision-making mostly has only restrictive aspects.

Be that as it may, the influence of legislation on business activities in general and on the business decision-making process is undoubtedly more comprehensive and more important than ever before. And the expansion of this influence is, of course, one way of augmenting the ethical element in business decision-making.

4.2. Social responsibility in international law

While sketching this positive picture of the widening of the social responsibility factor by way of national laws, I realise that we are also confronted with a less positive (or even reverse) tendency. As the world has become more and more interwoven, fewer and fewer problems can be coped with at the national level.

Even if I defer for a moment the introduction of multinationals into this discussion, this can easily be illustrated. For instance, pollution does not stop at national frontiers. If a factory badly pollutes the environment, a decision to locate it in a sparsely populated part of the Netherlands – but near the German frontier – would not be a very ethical decision if the part of Germany just across the frontier was densely populated.

These problems have to be solved at an international level. And unfortunately we cannot say that progress in this respect has been very impressive. International regulations have, of course, been made on a number of subjects. But by and large there are still (too) few results at this moment. This even applies to international organisations which have already made some progress towards integration, such as the EEC. Apart from the fact that international laws on the social responsibility factor in business decisions are not yet highly developed, the general dilemma of public international law plays a role too. For public international law, unlike national legislation, sometimes has very limited possibilities of enforcement, which can greatly reduce its effectiveness. Another problem with international legislation is that, until very recently most of the whole body of public international law was greatly influenced, if not formulated, by the developed nations. As a result, certain 'chapters' of international law were very unfavourable for the developing nations and therefore detrimental to their 'striving for human happiness.'

4.3. Social responsibility and the multinationals

The argument of the social responsibility element in international law affecting the behaviour of firms is closely related to (though not completely overlapping) the fervently discussed topic of the multinationals (MNC's). As Ramaer points out, MNC's have additional responsibility compared with private enterprises which operate in only one country. He 'translates' these additional responsibilities for the greater part as:[13]

'... respect(ing) the differences in cultures, laws and customs as between the countries in which they operate ...'

Combined with the previously mentioned problem of the lack of international legislation, this indicates the problems we are faced with when we talk about the 'ethical conduct' of MNC's. It is not enough for MNC's to comply with the laws of the countries they operate in. Often, these countries do not have the legislation needed to establish the 'social responsibility' standards which should lead to minimum standards of ethical conduct in business operations. But even if such legislation did exist they have not completely solved the problem because MNC's have many means of evading restrictive legislation by switching operations to other countries. Such – often undesirable – acts could be reduced by international legislation, but this is the very thing that is lacking at present. Public international law and international organisations do not have the appropriate instruments to cope with the transnational decision-making system used by MNC's.[14]

But even in this field some (minor) positive developments can already be noted: for instance the formulation of codes of conduct for MNC's by the United Nations, OECD and EEC.[15] As soon as these codes become part of public international law and their enforcement can be ensured, minimum ethical standards could be guaranteed.

4.4. Social responsibility and codes of conduct

As MNC's are mostly only restricted at the international level by codes of conduct drawn up by a number of organisations, and as it would be preferable for these

---

13. See J. C. Ramaer, 'Theses on man and private enterprise,' this volume.
14. See G. B. J. Bomers, 'Multinationale ondernemingen en gedragscodes,' *Intermediair 13th year*, Vol. 18, pp. 31–35; and by the same author, 'Multinational corporations and industrial relations: a comparative study of Western Germany and the Netherlands,' Assen/Amsterdam: Van Gorcum, 1976.
15. See P. Hesseling 'A moral interregnum for multinationals in the third world?', this volume.

codes to be made part and parcel of international legislation, the impression might be conveyed that such codes only exert a minor influence at present. Though this might be true in some respects, I believe these codes could, even if not yet incorporated in the body of international legislation, readily influence decision-making in such a way that the ethical factor is promoted. For example, decision-makers who want to promote the ethical factor in their decision-making process now possess useful backing for their argument in the mere existence of these codes.

The codes are formulated in organisations by delegations at a supra-national or national level (an exception being the ILO where both employers' and employees' delegations form part of the representation of the various countries).

Apart from these codes, business circles can also, and in actual fact do, formulate voluntary codes, for instance that are made at international level by the International Chamber of Commerce. The ICC formulated guidelines for international investment in 1972[16] which included articles on many aspects of all the four decision categories mentioned above.[17] That the ICC is focusing strongly on ethics in business is also illustrated by the establishment in 1976 of the Unethical Practices Commission.[18] It is evident that these codes formulated by firms themselves can very usefully supplement the minimum standards set by national and international legislation. The ICC codes have an international character and this is a big advantage in view of the international nature of economic life. Such codes of conduct could also be developed on a national basis or even on an industry basis. The problem with such codes is, of course, that debasement of the terms of competition has to be avoided. If a few firms, together covering only part of the market in one industry, intended to make a voluntary code of conduct, their intention would probably be thwarted by the mere existence of competing firms which could take advantage of the (draft) code to enlarge their market shares. Therefore a substantial majority of the firms operating in a particular industry is often a prerequisite for success.

But again, all these voluntary codes of firms at the international, national or industry levels can – even if they materialise only in part – help to enhance the ethical element in business decision-making.

16. See 'Guidelines for international investment,' ICC, 1972, Paris, adopted unanimously by the Council of the ICC.
17. See *inter alia* section 2.2.
18. See Information, ICC Members' Bulletin, No. 2/76.

5. Goals of firms and participants in the decision-making process

Two elements influencing the decision-making process are so self-evident that they first come to mind in a discussion on ethics in business: the goals of the firm, and the participants (individuals) in the decision-making process.

The attention these two elements generally draw is, in a way, quite natural. Ethics, as already stated, is a very personal thing and therefore decision-makers and a large part of the results and aims of their decision-making (i.e. the goals of the firm) frequently attract attention. There are several reasons why I did not start this article by discussing these two important elements. I thought it better to start by discussing the limitations within which firm's goals have to be formulated and within which decision-makers have to operate. To my mind, this puts the whole discussion in a realistic framework, without which a debate focused too sharply on these two elements – often with most emphasis on the decision-makers – would produce a lop-sided and over-pessimistic picture.

5.1. Goals of firms and ethics

For decision-making in business life, the goals of firms have an important and very specific influence. A closer look at these goals soon reveals that purely economic motives are not the only reasons for them. But even motives which seem purely economic can have ethical backgrounds, as Schreuder shows in his paper.[19]

The existence of multiple-goal structures has become a more generally recognised phenomenon. There is hardly anybody left who maintains that 'profit maximisation' is the only goal of business firms. Research and practice have demonstrated this over and over again.[20]

Because of these multiple-goal structures that presently exist within firms there is a very substantial possibility of also incorporating more ethical elements (in the form of social responsibility or ethics in a 'purer' sense) in business goals. One way might be the introduction of a Social bill of Rights as advocated by Hordijk.[21]

---

19. See H. Schreuder, 'The social responsibility of business,' this volume.
20. See for instance C. van Dam, 'Capital investment decisions: an introduction,' in: C. van Dam, *Trends in financial decision-making: planning and capital investment decisions*, Leiden, 1978, pp. 207–208. See also J. C. Ramaer, 'Theses on man and private enterprise,' this volume.
21. See A. Hordijk, 'Trade unionism and ethics,' this volume.

The introduction or strengthening of the ethical element in business goals may be of varying scope and have different grades of 'reality-value.' The scope might be classified as follows:

1. an 'ethical' goal which forbids the firm certain activities fully within the field of its activities;
2. an 'ethical' goal which forbids the firm certain activities slightly outside its 'normal' sphere of action;
3. an 'ethical' goal which obliges the firm to do certain things within the domain of its operations; and
4. an 'ethical' goal which obliges the firm to do certain things in a domain which outside its 'normal' sphere of action.

It will be evident that the different ways of incorporating ethics in business goals show a rising degree of difficulty in realisation ranking from 1 to 4. If one applies method 4, one should realise that this might even result in a complete, and in my opinion in most cases incorrect, reversal of the functions of states and firms in everyday life. In the past, many people supported the theory that business and government are completely countervailing powers: in business, only economic motives are promoted; the government has to promote social responsibility motives. A newer theory, by now dominant, recognizes that some social responsibility motives can also be found in business.[22] But when firms have to renounce certain activities inside their 'normal' spheres of action but instead have to perform activities outside their own spheres, this may prove to be the first step towards firms undertaking part of the work of governments or of public administration (of provinces or of townships). Incidentally, this tendency is also to be found in some recent trade union activities in the Netherlands.[23]

6. Decision-makers and ethics

Decisions in business ultimately have to be taken by individuals. Therefore, individuals are the last 'means' of promoting ethics in business decision-making. They do not, as already demonstrated, operate in a vacuum; laws, guidelines and goals set the framework within which they have to take decisions. However, because ethics in the purest sense of the word is such a personal thing, the

22. See H. Schreuder 'The social responsibility of business,' this volume.
23. For instance by accepting only a moderate increase in wages if the government reduces public spending on defence and increases aid to developing countries.

decision-makers themselves can introduce additional ethical elements (not yet included in social responsibility) into the discussion. Each individual of course needs and wants to live as much as possible in line with his or her ethical beliefs, both in private life and in other roles. But if a given role (in this case that of a decision-maker in business) provides no scope for this, it may pose a severe problem for the individual concerned. Therefore it is of essential importance that the laws, guidelines and goals under which decision-makers have to operate do not obstruct these individuals' input of the ethical factor. Earlier on in this article the reader's attention was drawn to the growing tendency to make the ethical element in business decision-making more important. Hence on the one hand, opportunities for individuals to introduce ethical arguments in the decision-making process are quite substantial. On the other, the lack of a *communis opinio* about ethics, even an ever-growing divergence about the 'content of ethics,' is liable to diminish the influence of the ethical thoughts put forward by each decision-maker.

The decision-makers' 'ethical' influence is of course needed most where 'minimum standards' (introduced by laws, guidelines or goals) are low or non-existent. This is one of the reasons why decision-makers in MNC's have a very great responsibility in this respect.

7. Conclusion

In this article I have developed a framework for the discussion of 'ethics and decision-making in business.' Though many different approaches to the subject could be put in this framework, it is of course impossible to dissociate its development entirely from the author's views. It is probably appropriate, therefore, for me to summarize my own attitude towards the subject at this moment.

The ethical aspects of firms' activities have drawn ever-increasing attention in recent years. The entire intricate problem can be split up into: *the factors* and *the actors*.

The factors are:
1. The growing interwoveness of the world as a whole. An ever-increasing world 'trade' in goods and ideas is leading to greater and greater interdependence materially and spiritually. By definition, this interdependence is becoming increasingly intricate (also because of the influence of technological developments which in turn often lead to environmental dilemmas, such as pollution, ... which can only be dealt with on the international plane: see sections 4.2

and 4.3). This is creating a *need* for a more ethical approach in business matters, as otherwise there might be too many unwelcome repercussions in various fields.

2. The growing awareness of ethical and social responsibilities as a result of a more sophisticated attitude by leading circles in the most advanced countries and cultures; made possible by the growth of prosperity in these countries (see section 3.3).

This *tendency* is leading to wider possibilities in this respect than ever before. The growing need combined with the growing tendency towards awareness are providing the actors with an unprecedented chance and opportunity.

The actors are:

1. The *decision-makers:* no research has ever proved that decision-makers in business are 'by nature' less ethical than other citizens. However, they work in an 'environment' in which material success (I am deliberately avoiding the more limited term 'profits') was until recently the predominant factor. Their 'environment' nowadays is defined by multiple-goal-structures, in which not just the economic motive is at a premium. This again is, of course, the outcome of the above combination of 'need' and 'tendency.' So the goals of firms can, and to some extent in fact already do, provide more scope for ethical considerations by individuals in decision-making positions.

   On the other hand, ideas of ethical values are scattered and rather divergent, and this will be reflected in decision-makers' conduct and acts. It may thus be dangerous to rely too much on these actors to improve the present situation.

2. The *firms* owing to the combined effect of 'needs' and 'tendency,' firms are, as I have just said, gradually turning away from purely economic motives and switching over to 'multiple-goal-structures.' Hence the firms' goals can, and to some extent in fact already do, open up possibilities for individuals to exert an influence on the basis of ethical considerations. Simultaneously, firms themselves can, and in practice do, bring about new, more comprehensive frameworks in the form of national or international guidelines (e.g. via the International Chamber of Commerce). As a one-step-higher authority they can exert substantial influence in this respect and/or leave decision-makers an ever-growing field where they can act 'according to their consciences' – although, again, divergent ideas on ethics may play a (disturbing) role. Hence my preference for rules, preferably binding upon an industry as a whole, and preferably (also) at the international level.

3. The *state:* the second-step-higher authority, again inspired by the combination of 'need' and 'tendency,' has more possibilities of enforcing

regulations. This may result in beneficial regulations but, applied in the extreme, may distort the firms' fields of action (see section 5.1).

4. Finally, *at the international level* – or on a supra-national plane – regulations can be made binding and all-embracing. This, for instance, is the only way to create the transnational framework for MNC's within which they will also have to observe certain minimum standards of ethical conduct.

Of course, no one expects all this to turn the (business) world into a community of saints. But I for one do hope and believe that well-considered and efficiently planned, concerted action, at both national and international levels, will make this world a better place to live in, with a better quality of life.

INDEX

* Italicized page numbers indicate the presentation of an entry which appears passim in following pages.